AF352457

THE CATHOLIC UNIVERSITY AS A SOCIAL PROJECT

THE CATHOLIC UNIVERSITY AS A SOCIAL PROJECT

REFLECTIONS ON JESUIT AND CATHOLIC HIGHER EDUCATION

MICHAEL J. GARANZINI, SJ, AND
JAMES P. McCARTIN, EDITORS

GEORGETOWN UNIVERSITY PRESS / WASHINGTON, DC

The publisher is not responsible for third-party websites or their content.
URL links were active at time of publication.

Library of Congress Cataloging-in-Publication Data

Names: Garanzini, Michael J., 1948- editor. | McCartin, James P., editor.
Title: The Catholic university as a social project :
reflections on Jesuit and Catholic higher education / Michael J. Garanzini
and James P. McCartin, editors.
Description: Washington : Georgetown University Press, [2026] | Includes
bibliographical references and index.
Identifiers: LCCN 2025006504 | ISBN 9781647126575 (hardcover) |
ISBN 9781647126582 (paperback) | ISBN 9781647126599 (ebook)
Subjects: LCSH: Jesuits—Education (Higher) | Jesuit universities
and colleges.
Classification: LCC LC493 .C38 2026 | DDC 378/.0712—dc23/
eng/20250617
LC record available at https://lccn.loc.gov/2025006504

♾ This paper meets the requirements of ANSI/NISO Z39.48-1992
(Permanence of Paper).

EU GPSR Authorized Representative
LOGOS EUROPE, 9 rue Nicolas Poussin,
17000, LA ROCHELLE, France
Email: Contact@logoseurope.eu

27 26   9 8 7 6 5 4 3 2   First printing

Printed in the United States of America

Cover design by Nathan Putens
Interior design by Westchester Publishing Services

*To the martyrs executed at
University of Central America in El Salvador in 1989
who continue to inspire the
Society of Jesus and Jesuit educators
to rededicate ourselves to the relevance and necessity of
Jesuit universities today*

Ignacio Ellacuría, SJ
Amando López, SJ
Joaquín López y López, SJ
Ignacio Martín-Baró, SJ
Segundo Montes, SJ
Juan Ramón Moreno, SJ
Celina Ramos
Julia Elba Ramos

TABLE OF CONTENTS

Introduction

Discerning the Future of Jesuit Higher Education

Michael J. Garanzini, SJ

T HE MISSION OF THE SOCIETY of Jesus—its gift to the Church, its charism—has been expressed for 450 years through a sustained commitment to the education of young people. This mission continues to this day in the hundreds of Jesuit institutions, at all levels of education, that promote character formation and excellence in learning around the world. Over the centuries, the superiors general of the Society have attempted to guide Jesuit institutions by reading the "signs of the times" and reflecting on how the Spirit might be calling these institutions to respond to changing needs by renewing and advancing our understanding of scholarship, of pedagogy, and of the ultimate goal of serving the common good by providing well-formed leaders to communities. If you ask educators in any Jesuit school, they will give you some version of this explanation of the purpose that drives the enterprise. From the first schools in Sicily and Germany in the fifteenth and sixteenth centuries to the present array of presecondary, secondary, and postsecondary institutions globally, the commitment to providing leaders for civic and ecclesial institutions has required a discernment process that is continuous and characterized by reflection undertaken among both the Society of Jesus's own leadership and its collaborators outside of the Society. That is, the Jesuits' own modus operandi requires dialogue and conversation, input from "the field," and ultimately an appropriate response from those with leadership responsibilities.

The collection of essays in this volume reflect on an address given by Father Arturo Sosa, SJ, the current superior general of the Society of Jesus and the past president of a Jesuit university in Venezuela. In 2023 he delivered the address in Boston to four hundred delegates from the 180 Jesuit higher education institutions around the world. Having gathered input from consultors and representatives from the six regional associations of Jesuit higher education, Sosa, like other generals before him, offered his reflections on how the concerns of our times ought to be understood and addressed in what we do and how we do it in Jesuit institutions. Sosa's reflections should not be understood as some final word on Jesuit institutions today. Rather, his intent—and the intent of this volume—is to invite a broad discussion of some of the most important issues facing Jesuit higher education in our times.

If their 450-year tradition has taught the Jesuits and their collaborators anything, it is that the continuation of our core mission requires three essential elements if we wish to be vital and relevant in the world: to remain rooted, adapted, and resourced. In this volume the reader will find reference to our rootedness in a shared tradition and history, especially when it comes to the major themes of faith, justice, and reconciliation that anchored Jesuit institutions in the fifteenth century just as they do in the twenty-first century. At the same time, the ongoing relevance of our institutions demands adaptation as times and circumstances change. Young people and the societies they inhabit are different from those in the past; for example, today they are structured—not simply influenced—by the growing impact of technology and broad access to rapid communication. Jesuit higher education today must adapt to such realities.

Finally, adaptation requires an ongoing practice of reflection—what in the Jesuit tradition we call "discernment"—on how we make use of our resources to advance Jesuit mission into the future. Who we teach, what we teach, how we engage the social and cultural challenges of our day must all be open for reexamination and rethinking with an eye toward how we appropriately use our resources to upgrade facilities, to recruit and retain top faculty, and to support those who cannot afford the kind of transformative education we propose to offer.

This volume opens with the text of Sosa's address. As is typical of past addresses on education by Jesuit leaders, Sosa weaves through his text a "composition of place." That is, he invites the reader to consider both the internal tensions in academic life today and the external forces that shape society and culture and impede economic and social progress for all, especially those at the margins. This dual consideration sets the stage for further reflection on the demands, including cost constraints, that come with serving all manner of students from the wide range of socioeconomic classes: We live within the tension created by a combination of shrinking resources and a call to share our resources more widely. To respond effectively to these tensions, he suggests, we must cultivate a culture of discernment within our institutions, thereby making use of the quintessential Jesuit tool for responding to the complexities of the present moment and preparing for an unknown future.

Sosa offers a simple definition of what he means by discernment: To discern is to "dispose oneself to be guided toward something new." This implies a willingness to let oneself be guided, to relinquish control. He admits that this is not the normal way we manage our institutions and our lives. In higher education particularly, the pace and the intrection of adjusting to change is the source of much anxiety and discussion, often leading to institutional inertia. But to discern, he says, we must allow ourselves to be open to the novel and the untried, to accept the fact that we are "pilgrims" on our way to something new.

If we are pilgrims, where are we headed? For Sosa, our direction should be marked by the four Apostolic Preferences of the Society of Jesus, which are themselves the product of a discernment process undertaken by the Society's members throughout the world. These four "directions," if you will, can be expressed in four questions: How might we advance the use of the Spiritual Exercises of St. Ignatius Loyola to help individuals find their true calling? How might we better accompany young people as they struggle for meaning and purpose in their lives? How might we better accompany those at the margins and share with them the rich material, social, and cultural benefits of our world? And finally, how might we better care for the Earth, our common home? A Jesuit college or university, Sosa argues, is one that sees these questions as critical to achieving their relevance in the world today.

Further, Sosa suggests that a Jesuit college or university is one that forthrightly addresses the forces that can disturb or derail our efforts. Specifically, he highlights three problems that we should take on with particular seriousness: superficiality, fragmentation, and instrumentality. Jesuit institutions, he says, must consciously and deliberately work to counter these three forces that can keep us from rigorous intellectual investigation, divide us into competing camps, and cause us to see human activity ultimately in transactional terms. Consequently, he also invites us to take up these critical questions in our discernment: How can we assist our students to resist the temptation of meaningless entertainment and of easy answers to complex problems? How can we help them to question their assumptions and prejudices and, in the process, to determine what values they wish to hold and act on in the world? How can we help students see connections among the academic disciplines and to use those disciplines to explore the complexities of contemporary problems? How do we help them resist the forces of ideology?

From here on in his essay, Sosa makes the case for a rich understanding of human nature that distinguishes a Jesuit education, and he emphasizes how eager our students are for something that speaks to their deepest hopes and desires, something that "upholds human dignity and contributes to fostering lives of meaning and purpose." This leads him to conclude that contemporary secular society is fertile ground for the Jesuit mission in education. Where forces of fragmentation exist, leaders in Jesuit higher education can—and must—lean into questions and methods that foster connection and integration. Where forces of instrumentality exist, they can—and must—work for deeper awareness, justice, and reconciliation, treating all with the dignity they deserve.

Ultimately, Sosa suggests that the academic culture of deconstruction, which has been influential for decades, has perhaps ironically promoted a context within which Jesuit higher education is ripe for the work of championing meaning, purpose, and possibility as opposed to diminishment, fragmentation, and disintegration. Further, he highlights two additional features of our current context that hold particular promise for us: intergenerationality and interculturality. Our institutions are gifted spaces for harnessing the benefits of multiple generations and multiple cultures. They are also natural places for experimenting with diverse viewpoints, diverse ways of constructing and sharing culture, and diverse ways of interpreting what constitutes a just society characterized by inclusion and dialogue. It is worth noting that perhaps because faculty, staff, and administrators swim in these waters every day, they may be unaware of how deeply this variety of generations and cultures enriches us and how readily it prepares us to create a world that supports all and reconciles diverse perspectives without the need to surrender uniqueness.

As he concludes, Sosa takes up the critical theme of the threat to democracy today. In fact, this threat may provide the greatest opportunity for us to leverage our mission to advance social cohesion and reconciliation. In this vein Sosa suggests that, as institutions and communities of marked cultural and generational diversity, Jesuit colleges and universities can play an important role in experimenting with approaches to democratic participation and encouraging democratic values. Thus, rather than calling on our institutions to be neutral regarding the political and social struggles of our time, he proposes that they become even more vital participants in the project of nourishing democratic life. Jesuit higher education is, in Sosa's mind, a *proyecto social*—a social force, a social experiment, a social project. Therefore, it is not neutral when it comes to the most important issues facing humankind. It stands for something. It promotes a vision of a just and inclusive society where the dignity of all is protected and honored. It opposes the forces that divide and that undermine human dignity. Of course, Sosa knows there are risks in undertaking such work. He also knows that we cannot be naive about the forces of resistance to our vision nor about the costs of doing so.

Following on Sosa's acknowledgment of the risks of undertaking Jesuit higher education today, the six essays presented after his address respond to his invitation to join in the "communal discernment of our future." Together they suggest that if we are to educate a new generation of leaders with a desire to build societies of inclusivity and intergenerational cooperation, all of us working in Jesuit higher education must participate in sober and deep discernment.

Eileen Burke-Sullivan's contribution considers Sosa's address in light of earlier interventions by three prior generals of the Society of Jesus: from Pedro Arrupe's 1973 address, which described the purpose of Jesuit education as educating "men [and women] for others," to Peter-Hans Kolvenbach's 2000 address, which called on Jesuit institutions to measure their success by the way their alumni act in the world, to Adolfo Nicolás's 2010 address highlighting the role of Jesuit colleges and universities amid what he called the "globalization of superficiality." Taken together, she argues, all four of the generals address the core problem of dehumanization that allows the powerful to consider the vulnerable (especially women and children) as objects or instruments to advance their wealth and pleasure. The following essay by James Hanvey, SJ, argues that Sosa's engagement with the tradition and language of the Spiritual Exercises models how Jesuit higher education can remain adaptive, dynamic, and generative in response to changing social and cultural circumstances. Hanvey also affirms Sosa's conviction that the spiritual practice of discernment, the foundational "way of proceeding" for Jesuits, will allow our campuses to become contexts in which we hope to "show the way to God" and assist young people in creating a hope-filled future.

Taking up the themes of intergenerationality and interculturality in Sosa's address, Eleonore Stump's contribution creatively draws on the work of the sixteenth-century Italian Jesuit missionary Matteo Ricci to show how contemporary humanists in the Jesuit tradition might effectively open themselves to the new and foreign and, in the process, discover truths that expand perception and understanding. Following on Stump's essay, Gordon Rixon, SJ, engages the theme of reconciliation and draws on his personal experience of working as a priest, theologian, and educator amid the clergy sex abuse crisis in Canada, highlighting the necessity of finding responsive and appropriate modes of engagement between the Jesuit tradition and the contemporary "historical dynamic" with all of its many challenges.

David J. O'Brien continues on the theme of history and reminds us that Jesuit higher education in the United States today is part of a long Jesuit tradition of accompanying people, young and old, into a "hope-filled future." O'Brien further highlights Sosa's resonance with Pope Francis's vision of engaging at the "heart of human history," and he emphasizes Sosa's suggestion that leaders in Jesuit higher education today may need to "let go of the reins," change our "focus and habitual ways of making decisions," and be open to "something new." The final essay, by Jennifer Abe, looks at some of the most difficult and disheartening concerns of today's students—social disconnection, stark inequality, global climate change, and political polarization—and asks us to consider how fortunate we are to have a dynamic Ignatian tradition to rely on as we aim to help our students face these problems and imagine a hopeful future together.

Considered alongside Sosa's address, these essays remind us of Jesuit higher education's capacity to approach the future with clear eyes on the world's problems, inadequacies, and injustices, as well as with a clear sense of our own responsibility to work toward a better world. Faculty, staff, and administrators at Jesuit institutions who are eager to cultivate their own hope as they embrace the vocation of serving the common good will find in Sosa's address and these essays a source of wisdom and an invitation to generative reflection.

1

Discerning the Present to Prepare for the Future of the University Education of the Society of Jesus

Arturo Sosa, SJ

With deep gratitude we can meet again after four years. Heartfelt thanks to those who have prepared this assembly with dedication, perseverance, and wisdom, and to Boston College, which welcomes us as sisters and brothers, taking care of all the details.

We have witnessed profound transformations in humanity during the four years that separate us from the Bilbao Assembly of 2018. We find ourselves in another stage of history, a stage that we sense but do not yet see with much clarity. We try to describe it as a "change of epoch," "the knowledge age" . . . because we perceive the depth of the changes that are underway in all dimensions of human life. The transformation came without giving us time enough to understand what was happening, much less to prepare ourselves adequately.

At the same time, we continue to experience in the daily life of the universities the tensions inherent in what they are. Tension between academic excellence and the integral formation of persons. Tension between rising to the demands of the day in infrastructure and technology and offering a quality education without any sort of social discrimination. Tension between the history, the tradition that has made the institution what it is, and the challenges of the present crisis that open up an uncertain future. These and many other tensions fill the minds, the hearts, and the daily work of those who have come together here.

This worldwide assembly has been proposed as an opportunity to discern in common the specific contribution of the institutions of university education under the responsibility of the Society of Jesus in the present moment of human history. What specifically they can be and do to help pave the way to a more just society with fraternal relations among persons, their cultures, peoples, and nations. So that the common good orients the decisions of global political economy. So that we move toward reconciliation with the environment, reestablishing an equilibrium in the use of natural resources that promotes not only the full life of all human persons but also life itself on planet Earth.

We seek a discernment that leads to shared decisions about what characterizes the universities, colleges, institutes and faculties that are members of this international Association. In other words, we seek to answer the question of what is particular to our institutions, what is that "special" or "unique" quality that characterizes their mode of inserting themselves in the present moment in the construction of the desired future.

We can ask the same question from another perspective: what can motivate a person or a family to choose to study, teach, do research, or work in a university that belongs to the International Association of Jesuit Universities (IAJU)?

To Prepare the Future Requires Discerning the Present

We run the risk of converting discernment into a comfortable label attuning us to a language that makes Jesuits smile and is music to the ears of Pope Francis. In fact, discernment requires accepting challenges that come to us from many angles of social life and from the sciences, challenges that often frighten us, with good reason.

To discern implies risk. . . . Risk-taking does not arise naturally from the dynamic of institutions that with great effort have constructed an identity, a successful way of educating and generating knowledge, a success that makes them proud and that is recognized in the circles in which they move and enjoy great prestige. To discern is to open oneself to something new.

The newness to which we open ourselves through discernment is radically different from the innovation that comes from scientific research or technological progress. It is a newness that is given to us, that does not follow from premises that we ourselves have put into place or from steps that we have taken along paths that we have chosen, designed, and constructed.

To discern, therefore, is to dispose oneself to be guided toward something new. It implies "letting go of the reins" to be led toward a destination we do not know, without relying on a road map that guides our steps. The characteristics of university institutions make it especially difficult to "let go of the reins." The institutions are designed to hold the reins firmly in hand and to control the road that is taken and the pace of movement.

To propose discernment in common as the way to face the future requires that we become aware of the resistances derived from the customary university dynamic. It requires consciously conducting a complex process to change the focus and the habitual ways of making decisions, avoiding the temptation to put the label "discernment" on what we already do because we are accustomed to it and it has gone well.

We have just closed the Ignatian Year 2021–2022. We have sought inspiration in the experience of Ignatius of Loyola in order to let go of the reins of our own lives, to be able to open ourselves to what is new, *to see all things new in Christ*, to allow ourselves to be led to new horizons. Ignatius applied to himself the image of the pilgrim. Following the same inspiration, we can imagine the IAJU, or better, the entire life-mission of the Society of Jesus, on pilgrimage, as a body with many members with different and complementary functions, taking to the road trusting in the Spirit that began the Society, guided it for hundreds of years, and promises to continue to guide it if we "let go of the reins."

From the faith that inspires the life-mission of the Society of Jesus and that opens us to work in harmony with many other persons and institutions that connect with it from other life choices, we know that the Holy Spirit guides through a particular way of acting in human history. The Spirit guides like a master who freely accompanies the processes of the disciples, respecting their liberty, following their processes patiently, adapting himself to the conditions of each place, moment, and person. The Spirit guides through what we might call the pedagogy of grace, opening our senses to the signs of the present that lead to the future object of our hope and our effort.

The "signs of the times," those signs that the Spirit gives with its action in history, are made manifest in the present. To learn to read the signs of the times is the discernment of the present that sheds light on the path to the future, a future that will be given to us if we elect to follow the path to which the signs point us.

A future consistent with the reason for being of the universities and educational institutes entrusted to the Society of Jesus requires, therefore, a careful discernment in common of the present. In this assembly we seek to move in that direction, examining the path traveled by the Association in the past years, deepening awareness of its necessity and committing the best available means to its realization.

The members of the IAJU are called to discern from the ground of the identity that is their reason for being, the principle and foundation of their mission, and the bond that unites them. Many universities have been examining this identity in recent years. We have been invited to return to its sources during this Ignatian year. It is the same spring that fed the long and complex discernment in common of the universal apostolic preferences of the Society of Jesus, and it still flows to make fruitful the apostolic works that put the preferences into practice.

Persons with a Life Full of Meaning

The identity of the institutions of university education joined in the IAJU begins with an integral vision of the human being. Therefore, we conceive of the university not as fragmented but as integrated. We propose institutions that offer the possibility of integrating the diverse dimensions of scientific, educational, and social activities.

An everyday university life that embodies and transmits that identity is, without doubt, an enormous challenge that requires paying attention to how ordinary campus activities are carried out; to how that identity is cultivated in the members of the university community and especially in its professors and administrators; to how decisions are made; to what incentives are proposed; to everything that constitutes the "success" of the programs and processes that are undertaken.

Like the whole system of higher education in the world, our institutions of university education are constantly threatened by three strains of virus with highly contagious variants: fragmentation, superficiality, and instrumentality. The illness that these viruses produce threatens the identity that unites us, inspirited by the charism that Ignatius expressed by using the phrase "to help souls" as the goal of the Society of Jesus, desiring to serve the mission of the Lord entrusted to the Church. "To help souls" is the Ignatian commitment that leads to integral attention to persons in all dimensions of personal and social life and in all that they need.

It is urgent, therefore, to discern what type of person we imagine as the fruit of the university experience that we propose. This is the central matter of our discernment. The human person needs to find meaning in his or her life and actions, the great actions and the small ones of every day. We propose "to seek and to find" the style of research, social action, and university education that is able to initiate and accompany personal and social processes that give meaning to life in all its dimensions, moving toward life in its fullness.

The spirituality that flows from the charism of the Society of Jesus understands the full life to be one that always seeks "in everything to love and to serve." That is how we conceive of "excellence." Through discernment in common, we propose to animate institutions that are excellent because the people who work, do research, teach, and study in them find the conditions to lead lives with meaning, lives that advance toward fullness.

Our university institutions are conceived in such a way that they offer space to accompany the processes of a great variety of persons who are living different moments of their lives, at the same time contributing, to the extent that they are able, to the transformation of the unjust structures of the societies in which they carry out their specific tasks as universities.

What we know as the "Ignatian pedagogical paradigm" is one of the most effective means to organize university institutions under our responsibility in accord with the identity that gives them meaning, the identity that leads them to offer opportunities to all their members to find the meaning of their own lives in relation to other persons and to the environment.

Those who are familiar with Ignatian pedagogy understand its close link with the Spiritual Exercises. In the Exercises Ignatius Loyola proposes a concrete way to experience the action of God in history and to discern the path to finding the meaning that makes life full. The widespread and responsible use of this precious instrument is, without doubt, within the reach of all our university institutions. Let us continue to use it, finding methods adapted to persons, times, and places. Let us take advantage of the experience to shape university spaces that incarnate the style proper to this identity.

One of the questions I often hear is this: is it necessary to share (Christian) religious faith to acquire the identity that is characteristic of our university institutions? In other words: does the path that leads to finding the meaning of personal and social life demand Christian religious faith?

The experience of our universities shows that full and meaningful lives are led by different persons with an amazing variety of personal religious, cultural, and political options. . . . This is one of the signs to which the proposed discernment must pay attention. Humanity is the common substratum of all persons, cultures, religious experiences, beliefs . . . The substantive nucleus of human fulfilment is the love that becomes *agape*, love that is lived in common, gathering humanity around it.

Sowing in Thirsty Soil

We experience in different ways the expansion of secular society as the space in which the immense majority of human beings live or will live. Some experience it as a threat, because processes of secularization have engendered bitter conflicts that have left deep wounds that are slow to heal and quick to reopen. Other environments have been totally captured by the principle that "anything goes" and suppose that it is enough to respect what each person thinks or feels in order to assure respect for my identity, ways of thought and religious faith. Vast sectors of humanity have been covered with the cloak of religious, ideological, or political fundamentalism, leaving little margin to think differently or to dissent.

Some, therefore, perceive secular society as ground that is parched and broken after a persistent drought. The truth is that the soil is thirsty. It offers us an opportunity to cultivate a life full of meaning.

We can characterize a mature secular society as "thirsty ground" because it has overcome ideological extremisms, religious and cultural sectarianisms, the hegemony of the market and the market's homogenizing dynamic that suppresses cultural diversity, depersonalizes, and relies on authoritarianism to sustain itself.

This thirsty ground is plural, with a wide range of different terrains and conditions suited to different and complementary crops. Secular society generates relationships that permit the exercise of human freedom in the different dimensions of life, opening spaces for human creation.

The mature secular society offers a new opportunity to live our identity and, from that identity, to make a significant contribution. Extending the image, we can water, sow, and cultivate in thirsty ground. The challenge for the discernment in common to which we are called at the present moment is to see clearly the signs of the opportunities that are opening to us in this new historical epoch.

Making the university a space of discernment helps to overcome the tendencies to fragmentation that exist in secular society. Our universities, located in the humanistic tradition of the pedagogy of the Society of Jesus, encourage processes that synthesize knowledge and integrate the dimensions constitutive of persons, societies, and the healthy relationship with the environment.

The humanistic tradition of the identity of our university institutions inspires the creation of knowledge through a multi-factored dialogue that includes the diversity of perspectives of all the disciplines that are cultivated in the university. This dialogue demands fluid and constant communication as a necessary means for building and maintaining the unity of minds and hearts that gives meaning to the institution. Equally, the transmission of knowledge as a fundamental dimension of the university's task contributes to the formation of well-integrated persons, committed to the transformation of society, agents of reconciliation who struggle for social justice.

We have accepted the challenge of inspiring and directing university institutions able to overcome the fragmentation of specialized scientific knowledge, through inter- and trans-disciplinary dialogue, inserted in a social context in which they are actively present with a universal vision and with awareness of forming part of a single, rich and varied humanity.

From the Experience of Intergenerationality and Interculturality

We can recognize the richness, the risks, and the potential of the future in two fundamental characteristics of humanity today: the diversity of cultures and the variety of ages that form the human population. To preserve and benefit from this richness we must face two complex and beautiful challenges: to advance toward interculturality with a deeply-rooted awareness of intergenerationality.

Recognizing cultural diversity as a richness leads us to join with a current that bases an interconnected or globalized world on multiculturality as a fundamental characteristic of the world of today and tomorrow. The creation of culture is an essential element of humanity, showing its capacity to open itself to what is new and better. This current runs counter to the imposition of a single worldwide market that subjects all human beings to the same scheme of production and consumption.

Because "the world is our home," as the first Jesuits said, every culture that dwells in it is our sister. That is why we want to go beyond multiculturality and open ourselves to interculturality as a process of human enrichment. The society in which we live is multicultural. So are our university communities. Interculturality is something more than the pluriculturality proclaimed by some of the nation states of the world. Pluriculturality recognizes the presence of different cultures in the territory of a state with laws that defend their existence and promote the coexistence of various cultures. This approach seeks to avoid the imposition of one culture over others in the same state or among nations as has occurred so many times in history and occurs even in our day in various parts of the world.

Interculturality, however, goes beyond the simple fact of persons of different cultures living together in a healthy coexistence. Interculturality begins with a step that is seldom clear and never easy. The first step is to develop a critical awareness of one's own culture that, recognizing its gifts and limitations, goes out to meet other cultures, contributing what one is and being enriched by exchange with the other.

The advances of the modern epoch made it possible to prolong the life of human beings and avoid the risks of illness and death from infancy until old age. In most of the world, life expectancy is much higher now than in earlier centuries. Many generations live together now. Generations with a great diversity of perceptions of what full human life is, should, and can be. The diversity of perceptions easily leads to generational "gaps."

The challenge of intergenerationality lies in the complex task of establishing an authentic dialogue within each generation and across generations. A dialogue that establishes spaces and conditions to listen to one another. A dialogue that, on the one hand, grounds fraternity among generations, and on the other is able to lead distinct generations to a commitment to seek the common good of humanity, including the reestablishment of a harmonious relationship with nature, with the environment and bio-diversity.

The member institutions of the IAJU—and the Association itself—are multicultural spaces in which many generations live together. Let us take to heart the challenges of interculturality and intergenerationality as opportunities to enrich the institutions and the persons who form the university community. Let us make this immense richness a patrimony to improve our contribution to the common good of humanity, struggling to make this world a home reconciled in justice.

The University, Politics, Global Citizenship, Reconciliation, and Peace

The proposal of universities that contribute to giving the full meaning to human life necessarily includes a political dimension. Through politics, meaning is given to social life. Drawing on the identity that grounds our university institutions, the integral formation of persons requires developing the citizenship of each person, of the university communities and of their institutions, expressed in a consistent commitment to the common good. As university institutions with local roots and universal vision, they are able to promote a global citizenship that works to overcome the great social gaps of today's world. In these universities, research and the transmission of knowledge are understood as effective instruments to contribute to orienting the geopolitical dynamic toward reconciliation and justice.

The characteristic identity of Jesuit university institutions leads to finding meaning also in public life. It demands thinking seriously, in the dynamic of the Ignatian *magis*, about how to better contribute to the deepening and expansion of democracy, which is threatened today even in those countries in which democracy has a long tradition and, one would suppose, a deeply-rooted consciousness of democratic values as the basis of political stability.

A recent essay by Moisés Naím[1] asks this question: Do those of us who come from a "democratic culture," convinced that citizens are the source of political power, governed by a system with checks and balances, understand the growing tendency everywhere toward autocracies that claim unlimited life-long power? Are we prepared for that?

I think I am not mistaken in affirming that the members of the IAJU are committed to political democracy and that you are also convinced that democracy needs the Humanities, because a democratic society seeks not only material prosperity but the integral development that comes from pursuing the common good.

We are witnessing a tendency that seeks to reformulate the basis of political legitimacy, diluting its democratic component. Naím classifies these forces as the three "Ps": populism, polarization, and post-truth. They are expanding in the most diverse nations of the world to such an extent that this can be considered a tendency with hegemonic possibilities.

There have been many studies, discussions, and publications about how populism empties of meaning the authentic exercise of the will of the people, how it weakens popular and civic organizations, how it eliminates the function of political parties as channels of alternative ideological-political programs to be decided in free elections by the citizens of each country. . . . Populism takes on a demagogic character that allows it to set aside the people in favor of the figure of an autocrat claiming to be the authentic interpreter of the will of the people and the only one who can implement the popular will through the use of political power.

Once power has been acquired, sometimes by taking advantage of the conditions of democratic regimes, the autocrat proposes to retain power indefinitely through the polarization of society and the support of followers who act like fans of a sports team. The autocrat is praised and defended in every circumstance, as fanatics defend the team they support forever. The discussion of ideas comes to an end because the autocrat expresses clearly the program of government and his word sets a course that cannot be doubted. His is the one voice and the one face of the government and of the state. The citizens and organizations that do not belong to his "fandom" are considered enemies to be neutralized or even eliminated.

The communications media strengthen this tendency when they focus political narrative only on the people who present themselves and act like the leaders of groups of fans. In doing so the media lose their character as mediators of political discussion and action. Development and expansion of so-called "social networks" has turned them into one of the most important ways of feeding polarized public opinion, displacing the mediating function of media like newspapers, magazines, radio and television that have a culture of balanced information, fact-checking, and verification of the authenticity of sources.

We face, then, given the characteristics and identity of our university communities, the question of how to enter helpfully into the world of social networks to convert it into one of the dimensions of the integral formation that we seek.

For the university that finds its reason for being in the systematic search for and diffusion of truth, it is a crucial challenge to confront the third "P" mentioned by Naím: the age of post-truth, of confused conceptualization and thought, of disinformation and the uncontrollable diffusion of fake news and conspiracy theories that distort reality.

Post-truth has such a capacity of manipulation that it can systematically block knowledge and diffusion of the truth about what is happening in the political arena. Post-truth converts the invention of reality into an instrument of domination and governance.

Autocratic regimes sustained by populism, polarization, and post-truth generate an atmosphere in which everything is always doubted except the word of the autocrat. The regime feeds uncertainty about what might happen in personal, family, or work life. Fear leads to political paralysis or to resignation in the face of what seems irremediable.

If at the same time the individualistic tendencies present in many cultures are exacerbated, then a stance against all politics can spread as an attitude toward public life. This is the most effective way to weaken the consciousness of citizenship, to lose the sense of actively participating in the search for the common good, and to expand the already grave threats to democracy.

As universities whose identity includes the commitment to the mission of reconciliation and justice, we have the enormous responsibility of helping to distinguish the truth from the falsehoods used to justify autocrats who present themselves as the only authentic defenders of the people. As exponents of democratic culture, we know that it is citizens who are aware, free, with contrasting ideas, capable of dialogue and of taking decisions within the horizon of the common good, who make possible the politics that leads to justice and fullness of life for all human persons, in harmony with the environment.

For our universities, the challenge of participating in public life and offering political formation to the members of the university community includes promoting governance based on truth, strong institutions, and the rule of law. We must contribute to a social environment that considers to be normal an ideological pluralism, a dialogue among alternative proposals. Above all, a commitment to create and maintain conditions that guarantee the possibility of alternation in the exercise of political power with scrupulous respect for the will of the citizens. In the international arena arrangements that permit the mutual defense of democracies and the diffusion of democratic culture should be promoted.

Remembering that our institutions depend for their operations on the generosity of benefactors, we should also recall that autocracies, and other powerful forces in many different social contexts, feed on dirty money coming from illicit activities or from corruption that turns public resources to private benefit. Many times they try to "launder" that money through donations to NGOs, charitable organizations, or institutions of social prestige. They might wish to include ours.

With and for Others

In recent years we have become more aware of the intrinsic relationship between the expression "for and with others," which we use so frequently to express our identity, and the educational task to which we are committed. We want to work in institutions and to be persons who are "for and with others." To do that, we must deepen collaboration in mission as an essential characteristic of our way of proceeding that follows from our identity.

Becoming a collaborator comes from hearing the call to participate in the mission of the Jesuit universities and electing to respond to the call as part of a body in which distinct vocations complement one another to contribute to the mission of Jesus Christ that has been entrusted to the Church, according to the charism of the Society of Jesus.

Collaboration is the way of proceeding of the apostolic body of the Society both within each apostolic work and among the different works that carry on the mission at the local, regional, and international level. Collaboration makes it meaningful to call ourselves a body and makes the body real in our daily life and work.

In the present moment of the history of the Society of Jesus we cannot even imagine educational institutions, or any sort of apostolic work, without plural teams in which people with distinct vocations of service join with the Jesuits. We also have experience with Jesuits collaborating in apostolic works initiated and directed by other institutions, groups, or persons.

What we understand as collaboration is a concrete way of living the ecclesiology expressed in the Second Vatican Council. The Church understands itself to be the People of God on the move, to which each person contributes according to his or her identity and talents. Collaboration is also a way to live universal fraternity and to labor side by side with people who, led by other religious beliefs, humanitarian options or desires to serve, join in working toward the same ends of reconciliation and justice. No one is superfluous. No one is expendable. We are all collaborators in the mission of Christ. That is a key dimension of our identity.

The collaboration characteristic of our identity includes the solidarity born of feeling ourselves to be brothers and sisters of all human beings, enriched by intercultural and intergenerational relationships, always ready to lend a hand to whoever needs it. Solidarity among persons and institutional solidarity are proper to our way of being and proceeding. Becoming men and women "for and with others" is the fruit of a well-educated solidarity. The university communities within our institutions are called to live that solidarity. They should be institutions with an organizational culture configured to that way of being and proceeding.

The International Association of Jesuit Universities finds its reason for being and the meaning of what it does in living and promoting collaboration and solidarity both within and outside the university institutions that form it. The goal is to take advantage as much as possible of the enormous potential for collaboration and solidarity that exists in the universities that form this network. We have started step by step down this path. As we go forward, we recognize the advantages of collaboration and solidarity. We are learning better ways to benefit from the resources that we have, resources that always seem scarce given the magnitude of the task.

The desire of the Society of Jesus is that this assembly renew the creative energies of the members of the IAJU so that we can grow as institutions that form persons who are integral and integrated, able to discern the present as long as they live, and committed to the search for social and ecological justice.

In the name of the Society of Jesus, I ask you to accept a heartfelt word of thanks for your commitment to the complex task of the university in such different contexts throughout the world. Please carry that gratitude to your university communities and continue to help us to be a body able in all things to love and to serve.

Thank you very much.

Note

1. Moisés Naím, *The Revenge of Power* (St. Martin's Press, 2022).

2

Placing Father Sosa's Vision for Jesuit Higher Education in Context

Key Interventions of Jesuit Leaders Since 1965

Eileen Burke-Sullivan

Introduction: The Deep Context

FROM THE MID-SIXTEENTH CENTURY TO the present the Society of Jesus has established works that seek to accomplish the foundational aims that the Society drew from the graces that God gave to St. Ignatius of Loyola. The missionary impulse—spreading the Gospel to the "ends of the earth"—the imperative of proclaiming the Word in various ways; celebrating the Church's sacraments; enabling individuals, families, cities, nations, and the world itself to seek reconciliation; and helping humans discover what joy God has in mind for each one and for all together were outlined as the purposes of the Society in the Formula of the Institute[1] written by Ignatius and the original companions. The emergence of the ministry of education was not explicitly named but quickly became an instrument for accomplishing these purposes. Today's universities are a primary work of the Jesuits, and every ministry of theirs must express the Society's mission. To engage in Ignatian discernment, however, one must have a clear grounding in one's call, one's charism for mission and of the "signs of the times"—the historical moments of development that bring us to the present moment in time. God acts and discloses desire in ongoing history as well as in the past. To discern spirits or God's call we have to know our historical context. How is the context to be read as works of God or of the "enemy" of human life? To make that judgment in grace we have to probe the recent context for grace and disgrace.

Father Arturo Sosa, SJ's, 2022 address on the future of Jesuit higher education was born out of a context that begins with the Second Vatican Council (1962–1965). Since then, Jesuits and their lay collaborators have been engaged in a prolonged effort to read what the Council called the "signs of the times," discerning over the course of decades how Jesuit higher education might speak to the most pressing needs and concerns of the day. In a particular way, the four Jesuit superior generals who have served since Vatican II have shaped this discernment through a series of seminal addresses delivered at key points in recent history. This essay attempts to contextualize Sosa's 2022 address by seeing it as part of a single trajectory that his predecessors helped to lay out in earlier addresses: Father Pedro Arrupe's 1973 address that described the purpose of Jesuit education as cultivating "men [and women] for others"; Father Peter-Hans Kolvenbach's 2000 address that called on Jesuit colleges and universities to measure their success by the way their alumni act in the world; and Father Adolfo Nicolás's 2010 address in which he highlighted the role of Jesuit institutions amid what he called the "globalization of superficiality."

These four addresses are informed by an array of sources. First and foremost, they are each inspired by the renewal efforts of Vatican II. They also reflect a commitment to honoring the ecumenical work of the whole Christian family and engagement with other faith traditions. The addresses further attend to the significant shifts in secular culture and technology and their impact on higher education. And of course, the context in which these addresses were offered was also shaped by various threats, some of them existential in nature: climate change, the expanding availability of weapons of war and mass destruction, the politics of fear, the globalization of the economy and the destruction of local economies, and the huge migrations of persons fleeing these and other dangers. At their heart, the four generals' interventions take up the core problem of dehumanization, especially in Western society and culture, which allows for a division of the world into extremes of wealth and poverty and enables the powerful to consider the vulnerable (especially women and children) as objects or instruments to advance their wealth and pleasure.

All of these things provide the context for asking the question: How does God desire the work of Jesuit higher education to go forward now?

The Inspiration of Vatican II: Returning to the Roots

Vatican II's "Pastoral Constitution on the Church in the Modern World" (*Gaudium et Spes*) was approved in the final days of the Council in the fall of 1965. Considered radical in many ways, this document explored some of the most challenging issues facing the world in the middle of the twentieth century and pointed to directions for the Church's focus in the new millennium. In the introduction to *Gaudium et Spes*, the Council fathers wrote:

> Inspired by no earthly ambition, the Church seeks but a solitary goal: to carry forward the work of Christ under the lead of the befriending Spirit. And Christ entered this world to give witness to the truth, to rescue and not to sit in judgment, to serve and not to be served. To carry out such a task, the Church has always had the duty of scrutinizing the signs of the times and of interpreting them in the light of the Gospel. Thus, in language intelligible to each generation, she can respond to

the perennial questions which men ask about this present life and the life to come, and about the relationship of the one to the other. We must therefore recognize and understand the world in which we live, its explanations, its longings, and its often-dramatic characteristics.[2]

To understand the trajectory of the Jesuit generals' interventions on the topic of Jesuit higher education since Vatican II, it is essential to know the historical context behind this vision in *Gaudium et Spes*. Modernity's rapid technological changes, its massive population growth, and the large-scale migration caused by violent wars and persecutions—especially the Holocaust—provided to the authors of *Gaudium et Spes* an invitation to articulate an updated understanding of the Church's essential purpose in the modern world. Further, rapid development of new scholarship on Jewish and Christian scriptures, liturgical practices, laws and customs, and moral awareness, both personal and corporate, helped to structure the conversation about updating, both during the Council and after.

Additionally, the Council's 1965 "Decree on the Adaptation and Renewal of Religious Life" (*Perfectae Caritatis*) directed communities of vowed religious, like the Society of Jesus, to review their original charisms (the gifts of the Holy Spirit that inspired and structured their shared lives and ministries) and discern how they could most effectively bring those charisms to bear in contemporary social and cultural contexts. This meant that they must commit to responding to God's self-revelation within history—an essential truth of the Incarnation, Jesus's taking on a human form as he entered into human history—and rather than depending on the way things had been understood or accomplished in earlier times, to consult the Holy Spirit who reveals God's presence and God's plan within the real contexts of each historical moment. The Jesuits had already begun such a process of renewal before the 1940 commemoration of the four hundredth anniversary of their founding, but it took on greater urgency in light of the vision outlined in *Gaudium et Spes*. Subsequently, the General Congregation 31 (1965–1966) and General Congregation 32 (1974–1975) took these mandates seriously, both in the election of their new superior general, Pedro Arrupe, and in setting a challenging plan for the renewal of Jesuit life and mission, including in higher education.[3]

As *Gaudium et Spes* indicated, the Gospels make it clear that the Church's mission is to take up the mission of Jesus and proclaim by action and relationship the Good News of God's saving love. Taking up this theme in the aftermath of Vatican II, the Synod of Bishops in 1971 asserted that, "Action on behalf of justice and participation in the transformation of the world fully appear to us as a constitutive dimension of the preaching of the Gospel, or, in other words, of the Church's mission for the redemption of the human race and its liberation from every oppressive situation."[4]

St. Ignatius of Loyola and his first companions asserted at their founding of the Society in 1540 that they were called to proclaim God's word, reconcile sinners, and help souls discover God, but to do so as a body constantly discovering where God is acting in the world. Their practice of "discerning" between spirits of God (good) and the enemy of human flourishing (evil) laid for subsequent generations of Jesuits and their collaborators a shared groundwork for decision-making that aims to discover what God desires in any given time and place. Likewise, Jesuits' essential work, which the first Jesuits referred to as "helping souls," increasingly came to be understood after Vatican II as "serving whole human persons," enabling all to flourish, both in this life and in the fullness of the Kingdom of God, through practices of spiritual growth and through communities aimed toward advancing justice. For Jesuits, the traditional ministries of preaching, teaching, and missionary work were therefore increasingly interpreted in light of the new historical moment in which they found themselves, a development that deeply informed the four seminal addresses by the superior generals.

Pedro Arrupe, SJ, Spain, 1973:
"Men [and Women] for Others"

Elected the Society's 28th superior general in 1965, Father Pedro Arrupe, SJ, would become a paradigmatic model of this new understanding of the Jesuit mission. As a young layman he had begun studies in medicine that he interrupted to join the Jesuits in 1927. Because the Jesuits were expelled from Spain amid the Spanish Civil War in 1932, Arrupe spent the majority of his years in Jesuit formation in other parts of Europe and the United States, completing his theological studies at Saint Mary's College in Kansas. During the early years of his formation he began reading *The Monumenta*, a collection of the writings of Ignatius and other early Jesuits, studying over seventeen large volumes that included personal journals, letters, and other documents collected and translated into Spanish at the end of the nineteenth century. Having been missioned to Japan in 1938, Arrupe was the Jesuit novice master in Hiroshima in 1945 when the United States dropped the atomic bomb there—an event that profoundly touched him and sustained his horror of violence for the rest of his life. Not surprisingly, when Arrupe spoke at a 1973 gathering of alumni of Jesuit institutions in Valencia, Spain, he had been well primed to offer a clarion call for Jesuit educators to prepare the next generation to spend their lives in the service of justice.

Although the address was mostly well received, it was controversial among those who were suspicious of *Gaudium et Spes*. Arrupe's message hewed to the line of Church teaching, grounding it in the Gospel and the commands of love of God and neighbor. Still, to critics it appeared to set out on a strikingly new path in terms of Catholic social teaching and moral theology by appealing to the sources of scripture and the ancient Church fathers in a way that had been uncommon in the period before Vatican II.

Early in his talk, Arrupe asked the alumni if they had been educated for justice in the way that the recent Synod of 1971 described it. He answered his own question: No, the Jesuits had not provided an education for justice. But, he went on to say, the Jesuits did have the tools to provide such an education because, from the beginning, they had something that prepared them for new discoveries and for adapting to new circumstances. "What is this something? It is the spirit of constantly seeking the will of God," he concluded. "It is that sensitiveness to the Spirit which enables us to recognize where, in what direction, Christ is calling us at different periods of history and to respond to that call."

Arrupe then described three attitudes, all of which demand commitment to the good of other human beings, that he saw as ideals to be adopted by those who experienced Jesuit education. First, they must learn to live more simply rather than spending great wealth for their own pleasure and comfort. Second, they must not take unjust profit from the goods of the earth or by (mis)using other human persons. Third, Arrupe insisted, graduates of a Jesuit institution should become an agent for change in the world they inhabit. With these three attitudes, he argued, Jesuit graduates will have been formed as "men [*sic*] for others," people filled with God's Spirit and prepared with various tools and skills necessary to make critical moral judgments and to alter the conditions of a sinful world.

Over subsequent decades, Arrupe's address would become a touchstone in the renewal of Jesuit higher education. Still, new questions and challenges would arise, including the challenge of sharing with non-Jesuit partners the responsibility of delivering Jesuit education and convincing these partners of its efficacy and methodology.

Peter-Hans Kolvenbach, SJ, United States, 2000: "Who Our Students Become"

In 1975 Father Arrupe opened General Congregation 32 (GC 32) to continue the internal reform efforts spurred by Vatican II and to explore Jesuit mission in relation to the "problems of contemporary change." This gathering would be the culmination of a multiyear process during which Jesuits throughout the world were called on to embrace the "Ignatian spirit," reflecting and conversing together about the mission of the Society in the contemporary world. As Arrupe understood it, this prolonged process would model the process of conversion among students at Jesuit institutions; it would begin with reflection on the personal level and move to reflection at the communal level, a process by which graduates, individually and communally, could become agents for change of the world. A linguist teaching in the Jesuit-sponsored Université Saint-Joseph in Lebanon, Father Peter-Hans Kolvenbach, SJ, would represent the Province of the Near East at GC 32, and he would later bring that experience into his leadership as superior general from 1983 to 2006 and his own vision for Jesuit higher education.

Kolvenbach, in the first section of his address to leaders in U.S. Jesuit higher education assembled at Santa Clara University in 2000, centered his comments around one of the key documents issued by GC 32, a decree entitled "Our Mission Today: The Service of Faith and the Promotion of Justice." This decree, Kolvenbach said, arose from Jesuits' growing realization that

> the entire Society of Jesus, in all its many works, was being invited by the Spirit of God to set out in a new direction. The overriding purpose of the Society of Jesus, namely "the service of faith," must also include "the promotion of justice." The new direction was not confined to those already working with the poor and marginalized in what was called the "social apostolate." Rather, this commitment was to be "a concern of our whole life and a dimension of all our apostolic endeavors." So central to the mission of the entire Society was this union of faith and justice that it was to become the "integrating factor" of all the Society's works, and in this light "great attention" was to be paid in evaluating every work, *including educational institutions.*[5]

Some of the most corrupt citizens of Beirut during his time there were graduates of the Jesuit university, Father Kolvenbach pointed out, and he added that the politically tenuous situation in the Middle East made a struggle against sinful, unjust structures very dangerous. In the immediate aftermath of GC 32, he said, few Jesuits really understood the implications of the 1971 Synod's document—or even of Ignatius's call to be a companion of Jesus on his road to torture and death on the cross. Perhaps this general lack of understanding was what spurred Society's leaders at GC 32 to take what Father Kolvenbach termed a "radical stand," coining and affirming the dual formula "the service of faith and the promotion of justice."[6]

Reflecting back a quarter century later, he saw that Jesuits had embraced and integrated this formula and its implications into their mission and their very identity. The service of faith, from the foundations of the Society in 1540, marked the fundamental identity of its work and entailed a deep and loyal commitment to Church teaching, including the teachings of Vatican II and the Synod of Bishops that followed. Many Church leaders would later be frightened by the more radical implications of this dual approach to faith and justice. Still, Kolvenbach reminded his audience, the service of faith and the promotion of justice was a theme directly drawn from both the Old and New Testaments and central to Jesus's way of life. Further, he suggested, all justice work for a Jesuit must be initiated by the Lord's labor in events here and now. A deeper sense of the theological and pastoral underpinnings of such an understanding of the service of faith, Kolvenbach concluded, would have made the logic of the promotion of justice more obvious, preventing sometimes divisive misunderstandings even among Jesuits themselves over the preceding quarter century.

In the aftermath of GC 32, the higher educational mission of the Society became an object of criticism among many Jesuits because it only rarely seemed to involve direct work among the poor. Some even went so far as to suggest that Jesuits should divest themselves from higher education and shift their energies to ministries that had a clear and direct impact among the poor. By 2000, however, such calls died out as universities and colleges better practiced their role in forming men and women for others and becoming places of authentic growth in learning and in developing skills and practices desperately needed for the promotion of justice in the world. Jesuit universities in Central America led the way in considering how Jesuit higher education goes beyond teaching and research to being a "social project," engaging local, national, and international communities to develop strategies for establishing a more humane world. Higher education, in this rendering, provided the critical means by which individuals and communities could change unjust social structures.

Throughout the last quarter of the twentieth century, an array of historical events also contributed to advancing support for the "service of faith and the promotion of justice" in Jesuit higher education. For example, a series of high-profile murders in El Salvador—first of Archbishop (now Saint) Oscar Romero in March 1980; then of three U.S. missionary sisters and a lay collaborator in December 1980; and finally of six Jesuits and two laywomen at the University of Central America in 1989—helped to stir the conscience of Jesuits and their collaborators in higher education around the world. In North America, the prolonged struggles against racism and sexism also helped to shape reflection about the purpose of Jesuit higher education, especially as the student populations at U.S. Jesuit institutions became more racially diverse and as women enrolled at Jesuit institutions in much larger numbers thanks to the expansion of coeducation. Moreover, major historical developments like the fall of Soviet communism, the globalization of markets and popular culture, and a rising of consciousness about environmental destruction and global climate change all contributed to building the context in which Kolvenbach spoke in 2000—a context in which educators were wrestling with how to make their education relevant to the changing times.

Twenty-five years after he delivered it, Kolvenbach's address is most often remembered for the statement, "The real measure of our Jesuit universities lies in who our students become." With this in mind, perhaps it is time we listened more closely to a critical question he asked of faculty in his address: "'When researching and teaching where and with whom is my heart?' To expect our professors to make such an explicit option and speak about it is obviously not easy; it entails risks. But I do believe . . . [this] to be our defining commitment [in Jesuit higher education]."

Adolfo Nicolás, SJ, Mexico, 2010: Resisting the "Globalization of Superficiality"– Embracing "Universality" and "Learned Ministry"

Like Arrupe, Father Adolfo Nicolás, SJ, was born in Spain but would spend many formative years in Japan, and also in the Philippines, before being elected as the 29th superior general in 2006. Among the important developments that would take place during his leadership was the 2013 election of Jorge Mario Bergolio, SJ, as Pope Francis. Critically, both Nicolás and Bergolio experienced formative years as Jesuits under Arrupe's leadership, and together they took as their way of life a formula offered at GC 34 in 1995:

> Today we realize clearly:
> No service of faith without
> > promotion of justice
> > entry into cultures
> > openness to other religious experiences
> No promotion of justice without
> > communicating faith
> > transforming cultures
> > collaboration with other traditions . . . [7]

In his 2010 address to leaders from Jesuit institutions around the world who gathered in Mexico City, Nicolás reaffirmed the society's commitment to ministry in higher education but highlighted the necessity among those engaged in this work to take account of rapidly changing social and cultural contexts. By this time many Jesuit institutions had come to take for granted a commitment to educating men and women for others and preparing them to be agents of justice in the world. But the changed context of 2010, Nicolás said, required taking up three themes into the future: "First, promoting depth of thought and imagination. Second, rediscovering and implementing our 'universality' in the Jesuit higher education sector. Third, renewing the Jesuit commitment to learned ministry."[8]

With regard to the first theme, Nicolás identified a negative effect of globalization that he termed the "globalization of superficiality." He saw at the foundation of this superficiality the rise of social media and of internet-based search engines—developments that undermined engagement in the work of serious, critical thinking and that, he suggested, must be countered through a renewed commitment to "depth of thought and imagination." Such a loss of depth through the advance of superficiality, Nicolás suggested, dehumanizes both the actors who succumb to superficial thinking and the "others" whom they act on, almost guaranteeing the advance of serious injustice, both personal and structural, and undermining efforts to prepare alumni whose core interests and concerns are "for others." So Nicolás did not abandon Arrupe's insistence on educating for justice as articulated in 1973. Instead, echoing Kolvenbach's challenge to faculty in 2000 to reflect on how they shape their students, he called for a deepening of this reflection so that the contemporary threats to deep understanding and deep connection to others can be properly understood in light of the Jesuit commitment to "the service of faith and the promotion of justice."

I want to suggest that one contemporary example of the kind of superficiality that Nicolás spoke about is that some political forces in the United States are moving strongly today to outlaw critical thinking in public schools in several of the states. Such a move is a product of the fear, shared by many in our culture of superficiality, that critical thinking will furnish serious foundational research that undermines the self-security of fundamentalist thinking and enables people to dismiss evidence contrary to their superficial understanding. Indeed, such superficiality not only affirms fanaticism and divisive ideologies, but it also allows for the dehumanization of others who may not be valued, understood, or even seen from a superficial perspective. When we find ourselves in such circumstances, Father Daniel Hendricksen, SJ, has argued, we should see ourselves as invited to embrace an approach to engagement that exercises both our intellectual and our affective dimensions. Such an approach has the capacity to bring a person on "a pilgrim adventure that wanders meaningfully through personal construals and experiences and deepens thoughts and feelings . . . breaking down the rational buffers that suppress sentiments, distrust intuitions, and prevent imaginations." In embarking on this adventure, Hendricksen concludes, we can respond to Nicolás's invitation and thus ensure that the "tools of analysis, reflection, and discernment" remain embedded not only in Jesuit higher education but also in our graduates, who we hope will become well-formed critics of superficiality.[9]

Nicolás's second challenge—"rediscovering and implementing universality"—requires that we attend to the essential message of Jewish and Christian scripture that our world is one world, that every aspect of Creation flows from the same loving source, and that every human person has the same dignity and worth as every other human person. Furthermore, every Jesuit institution of higher education is part of every other Jesuit institution of higher education, and rather than isolating or competing with one another, we must develop ways of collaboration that build up the Jesuit common mission, not any one institution's glory. This does not mean that we should not compete in the sports arena, for example, or have friendly rivalries. Nor does it mean that a certain school that serves in a particular social and cultural context should be exactly like a Jesuit school in another context. Rather, it means that we must find ways to build up each other and the network of Jesuit institutions to better serve the world. Under Nicolás's vision, collaborative, inter-institutional programs such as Jesuit World Wide Learning (JWL.org)—whose mission is to provide high-quality, university-level learning "to communities at the margin of societies"—would become the norm so that students living in refugee camps in Africa, for example, have access to the best possible education that the wealthier West can provide. Likewise, Jesuit colleges and universities in the United States could be greatly enriched by drawing on resources and perspectives that Jesuit institutions in India, for example, provide to their students. Such acts of collaboration could be understood as part of the "pilgrim adventure" that Hendricksen imagines, enabling students (and faculty) to ponder deeply on that which is not part of their immediate experience. We have far to go in the "me-first" United States before we can name great success in collaboration of all kinds. But through such adventures, we have the capacity to learn to become far better collaborators than competitors—and in doing so embrace Nicolás's call to rediscover and implement our universality.

The third theme Father Nicolás took up is what he calls "learned ministry." By this he meant what in the past was often called the "intellectual apostolate"—otherwise known as undertaking research designed to shed new light on human experience and on the natural world. For Nicolás, learned ministry meant making discoveries that would ultimately illuminate the "depth" of these objects of study and their participation in "universality" but also how faith can be authentically lived within the secular context of the twenty-first century. Consequently, Nicolás invited Jesuit institutions to engage with a secularity that is often not just neutral to faith but indeed may be adamantly opposed to it. And his invitation was to produce not only research allowing people of faith to understand the secular world but also research enabling secular people to gain a deeper understanding of why so many, both in the past and in the present, have experienced faith as a compelling dimension of their lives. Moving beyond the invitation to engage with respect and affection across many faith traditions, he invited those in Jesuit higher education also to engage with respect and affection with people of no faith. Thereby, Jesuit institutions would be positioned to break down the contemporary barriers between faith and secularity.

Nicolás takes the discussion of his key themes far deeper than the summary above can cover. In the end, however, it is important to affirm that his 2010 address expands on themes that Arrupe laid out in 1973 and that Kolvenbach took up in 2000—themes that speak to the ongoing discernment of the "signs of the times" and that also enshrine "the service of faith and the promotion of justice" at the heart of Jesuit higher education, making this dual formula the enduring measure by which Jesuit universities determine their raison d'etre.

Father Arturo Sosa, SJ, United States, 2022: The Importance of Ignatian Discernment

Elected superior general in 2016, Arturo Sosa is a Venezuelan who entered the Society of Jesus in 1966 and later served as a political science faculty member at two Venezuelan Jesuit universities and as the longtime editor of a journal of politics and social ethics. Sosa's 2022 address fits well within the trajectory of earlier interventions by Arrupe, Kolvenbach, and Nicolás, taking up nearly all of the themes they had covered. But he also drilled down on one theme that, to a certain extent, remained in the background of earlier addresses—namely, the theme of Ignatian discernment.

Indeed, between Nicolás's 2010 intervention and Sosa's 2022 address, a number of critical events and trends arose—events that would present major challenges to those seeking to discern a way forward for Jesuit higher education. During those years, a resurgence of racism and its heinous effects became the focus of much attention across the globe. A politics of backlash against naming and fighting racism likewise emerged, in some cases undermining democratic forms of government and causing remarkable violence. Similarly, during the decade before

Sosa's address, there was a massive explosion of migration due to poverty, violence, political persecution, and climate change, and tens of millions found themselves on the move simply to find a safe home. Widening economic differences, with the rich becoming much richer and the poor becoming much poorer, also picked up speed and power. The world experienced an on-going expansion of social media and other means of rapid (and often vapid) communication, deepening the dehumanization process that Nicolás had highlighted. Of course, the global climate crisis only worsened in its capacity to threaten planetary life in all its forms—yet another root source of injustice and dehumanization, since the poor experience its effects incrementally more than the rich who contributed so much to its cause. And most certainly, the COVID-19 pandemic, which continues to take lives despite being thought to be "over," emerged as a challenge to nearly every human relationship.

So, the question is: How does Jesuit higher education continue to pursue its mission in the context of these and other rapidly changing "signs of the times"?

The answer, of course, begins with the practice of Ignatian discernment, which is not just about making decisions with accurate data or developing a viable strategic plan. Rather, Ignatian discernment is the intricate work of discovering the greatest good, God's desire for us at this time—a work that demands all the skills and all the themes taken up by Jesuit superior generals over the past sixty years. Ultimately, discernment requires a conviction that Ignatius and the early companions found so radically important and that remains central to Jesuit life and ministry—the conviction that there is a God who loves us. Among those truly committed to Ignatian discernment, the Spirit of God leads them to new places on a pilgrimage not of their own planning, making use of the gifts and talents of those who generously dispose themselves to "let go of the reins," as Father Sosa puts it, and who allow themselves to be drawn where they previously might not have imagined they could go.

Each year, I collaborate with a mission officer at another Jesuit university to take faculty and staff from both of our institutions on a pilgrimage path in Spain along which Ignatius was led. These pilgrims are a microcosm of the community at a typical Jesuit institution in the United States today: some have a deep Christian faith; some come from other faith traditions; some have no faith, but a love for the Jesuits and their way of proceeding; some are young and not even sure how faith could fit into their busy lives. On these journeys, things tend to happen differently than we had planned. As members of the group begin to share their inner lives, their imaginations, and their experiences, they often discover something entirely new—a vocation to serve at a Jesuit institution. On these journeys, my collaborator and I have discovered that those who participate come back different, prepared anew to teach, to lead, to guide others, to think about the future of Jesuit higher education.

As I reflected on Sosa's address, I was struck by the trajectory that Jesuit universities are on. It is a trajectory that emerges from a guiding sense that every person matters, that the created world matters, that the values expressed so deeply in our teaching and research matter. With this in mind, we in Jesuit higher education who give ourselves over to Ignatian discernment need to be open, to be willing to be surprised. We also need to prepare ourselves by exercising the gifts of imagination, research, asking deep questions, and dialoguing with others whom we have not known or valued in the past. We need to lean on the historic strengths of Jesuit education: the humanities and arts; the Ignatian Pedagogical Paradigm; the value of *cura personalis*; and the enduring call, shared with Ignatius and his companions, to reconcile persons, groups, cities, and nations. We who commit to Ignatian discernment must recognize that it requires both the gift of listening and the gift of risking. And in the end, we must be ready to do it again and again, because change is constant and, in our world, it is also rapid.

In his reflection on discernment, Sosa points out that the Spirit will not solve problems by some sort of alchemy or magic but instead by using our gifts, our strengths, and even our weaknesses to help us determine how best to engage the problems of our world. Undoubtedly, along the way we will have to suffer the loss of some things and take up new approaches in our work to align Jesuit higher education with the service of faith and the promotion of justice. But in the end this is what is required of us who participate in the graced and privileged ministry of Jesuit higher education.

Notes

1. The Formula was written by the first fathers of the Society and presented to Pope Paul III in 1539, requesting official status as a religious order of the Catholic Church. In 1540 Pope Paul established the order by the promulgation of *Regimini militantis Ecclesiae*. For a brief historical background read John O'Malley, SJ, *The First Jesuits* (Cambridge, MA: Harvard University Press, 1993), 2–8. For a thorough study of the document an excellent resource in English is Joseph Conwell, SJ, *Impelling Spirit* (Chicago: Loyola Press, 1997).

2. *Gaudium et Spes* (The Church in the Modern World). Final Constitution of Vatican II, promulgated December 7, 1965. #2. https://www.vatican.va/archive/hist_councils/ii_vatican_council/documents/vat-ii_const_19651207_gaudium-et-spes_en.html

3. "A general congregation is the highest authority. The ultimate governing body in the Society of Jesus. It is also the most representative instance of the Society's current understanding of itself, its life and its mission in the context of its Constitutions, its history, its spirituality, and the world in which it seeks to serve the Lord." John W. Padberg, SJ, ed., *Jesuit Life and Mission Today: The Decrees and Accompanying Documents of the 31st–35th General Congregations of the Society of Jesus* (St. Louis: Institute of Jesuit Resources, 2009), xi.

   Congregations discern and elect a new superior general at the death or resignation of the previous one (generals have historically been elected for life) and adapt the work and life of the Society to the times in which they are called. Such meetings are held irregularly and only at need. As of 2024 there have been 36 general congregations in the history of the Society from the first in 1558, after Ignatius's death (Fr. Diego Lainez, 2nd superior general), to 2016 after Adolfo Nicolás resigned for serious health reasons. Arturo Sosa elected 31st superior general.

4. "Justice in the World" from the 2nd World Synod established by the Second Vatican Council. Decree 2. christusliberat.org/journal/justicia-in-mundo-justice-in-the-world/.

5. Peter-Hans Kolvenbach, SJ, "The Service of Faith and the Promotion of Justice in American Jesuit Higher Education," Part I, 2. *Santa Clara Lectures* (2000). https://www.scu.edu/media/ignatian-center/santa-clara-lecture/Kolvenbach.pdf

6. Kolvenbach, "The Service of Faith."

7. Padberg SJ, ed., *Jesuit Life and Mission Today*, GC34. Decree 2 "Servants of Christ's Mission." #19, 529.

8. Adolfo Nicolás, SJ, "Depth, Universality, and Learned Ministry: Challenges to Jesuit Higher Education Today." Introduction. (2010).2. https://unijes.net/wp-content/uploads/2019/06/NicolasSJ.JHE_.April23.20102.pdf

9. Daniel S. Hendrickson, SJ, *Jesuit Higher Education in a Secular Age: A Response to Charles Taylor and the Crisis of Fullness* (Washington, DC: Georgetown University Press, 2022), 13–14. Father Hendrickson's text is a philosophical response to Charles Taylor's landmark book *A Secular Age*, wherein the author seeks for "fullness," a concept of human flourishing in a world that has too often abandoned or trivialized religious thought in seeking genuine humanity in light of meaning in life and work.

3

The Jesuit University

Called into Mission

JAMES HANVEY, SJ

Introduction

FATHER GENERAL ARTURO SOSA'S ADDRESS represents a significant and wide-ranging exploration of the fundamental mission of the Jesuit university today. It comes at an important moment for higher education in general and for the Society of Jesus's work in particular. Most Jesuit universities in the United States are at an inflection point. The vision of a Jesuit university offered by Father Sosa is broad and challenging. It understands the university to be a source of transformation, not only for students but for the wider society it serves. The breadth of this vision will be attractive to some and questioned by others. On the surface, it could be read as the program for a university in the liberal humanist and democratic tradition. It might even be accused of utopianism. If the address generates a lively critical discussion around these themes, then it will have already made a significant contribution. As one would expect from the superior general of the Society of Jesus, the address presupposes and is shaped by the Gospel and Spiritual Exercises of St. Ignatius. Throughout the history of the Society, rather than proving to be a narrow lens, the Exercises have shown themselves to be adaptive, dynamic, and generative. Together with the other visionary founding sources of the Society, implicitly and explicitly, the Exercises have shaped the practice of all its apostolic enterprises.

In themselves these sources bear witness to the fact that, from an early stage, the Society saw that education is itself a work of transformation. Education is our hope in the future and our commitment to it. This hope is not only the expression of an optimistic humanist tradition. For the Society, the commitment to education is a recognition that the future is not determined by human desire or vision alone; it is God's future which is already at work in history. From this perspective all education is a participation in, and service of, the Divine economy of salvation. For this reason, in any authentically Jesuit work "mission" is never rhetorical or aspirational but primarily theological. As such it has an incarnational dynamic ensuring that mission never remains abstract but constantly seeks to be expressed in the concrete forms, structures, values, and relationships of every apostolate. Therefore, we must expect that it will be seen and tested in the daily life of our colleges, the reality it produces and the lives it shapes. For this reason, too, intrinsic to the actual expression of mission is the habit of reflection or discernment. Discernment must be integral and implicit in mission if the work is to be an "instrument in God's hands," as the Jesuit Constitutions describes its ministries.[1] Both mission and discernment are clearly present in the Father Sosa's address. I believe they constitute the hermeneutical presuppositions of his other themes, and for this reason it will be useful to explore them further before turning to the central aspects of his speech.

Three Dimensions of Mission

Obviously, the word "mission" is not the exclusive possession of the Society of Jesus or the Catholic Church. In fact, its extensive use in so many fields renders it problematic. As we know, the same word does not always carry the same meaning. Indeed, it can mask uses and understandings that are at variance with one another.

In contemporary society, it is commonplace for organizations to speak about their "mission." In visiting the website of any university or company, it is guaranteed that you will find a mission/vision statement: a self-constructed presentation of identity, purpose, and product. Apple, one of the world's most successful organizations, has a mission/vision statement, vowing "to bring the best user experience to its customers through its innovative hardware, software, and services." It appears modest and understated, but in 2019 Tim Cook set out Apple's transcendent purpose, almost their own corollary to the "Principle and Foundation" in the Spiritual Exercises: "We believe that we are on the face of the earth to make great products."[2] Apple would have us believe it is not just a highly successful design and production company that includes an aesthetic experience, but that it offers a whole technological and design soteriology! In order not to be seduced by mission marketing and hyperbole, we who work in Jesuit apostolates or have responsibility for them need to be clear about what we mean when we speak of mission. From Jesuit sources, I think it is possible to identify three dimensions that characterize the experience and understanding of mission. Attentiveness to them is important not only in articulating what our mission is but in how we preserve and develop it.

1. Mission is not something we create. It is something we receive.

In the context of a Jesuit apostolate, mission is not our own self-construct and choice of purpose; it is a participation in Christ's mission.[3] In this respect, the mission is greater than any one institutional expression and will be experienced as such. It is always something that we are living and discovering through experience and reflection but can never exhaust. The principle is summed up by Paul: "caritas Christi urget nos" (2 Cor. 5:14)—the inexhaustible and ever-expanding love of Christ drives us on to an ever-deeper encounter with the world and its needs. It is through the Church that we receive Christ's mission; therefore our mission is not, nor can it ever be, something separate from the mission of the Church. It is both an expression of it and a service to it. This critical marker distinguishes the Society and its apostolates from all other corporate organizations.

That mission is received and not invented imposes its own responsibility: not to lose sight of Christ and to remain always faithful to the Church.[4] It is a mission that is necessarily committed to the way of the cross.[5] It is not by accident that the founders of the great religious orders of the West and their spiritual traditions are all marked by the cross and its countercultural wisdom. As Ignatius's vision at La Storta indicates, the Society not only desires to be placed with Christ in his mission, "under the banner of the cross," it is also committed to Christ's means of fulfilling his mission. It is the way of the crucified Lord, vividly expressed by the "Two Standards" in the Spiritual Exercises.[6] This "divine foolishness" which subverts all our notions of power and success applies as much to our institutions as it does to persons. Too often we can be tempted to make this dimension of our mission and its values into a "value-added" marketing tag rather than a call to do the deep re-imagining that discipleship calls for. This will always remain a challenge to our universities that find themselves in competition with powerful and secular academic institutions.

2. The mission is real and concrete.
It always has an "incarnational form."

Mission responds to "times, places, and persons." In this respect, while we have considerable adaptability about the means, we do not define or determine the end.[7] It is Christ who does that. Every Jesuit mission lives in the dynamic of seeking the best means to respond to the mission it has received. In some sense it will always experience itself as living beyond its means, for the mission it receives can only be experienced as *semper maior—always greater.* At this point we experience our necessary poverty, for in mission we will always be living and working beyond our human and material means. For this reason, the actual experience of mission will proceed from a "spiritual poverty," but this is the lived recognition of the priority grace in all that we do. From this Marian aspect flows our commitment to evangelical poverty—institutional as well as personal—that is vital to our evangelical freedom and its witness. It is integral to the universality of our mission in which no one or no group has a privileged place except those who have the greater spiritual, material, and social need.

3. To be faithful in all we do, we must be a continuously reflective and discerning community. Of all the resources available to us for this mission, the Spiritual Exercises remain the principal one.

The Spiritual Exercises underpin all that is in Father Sosa's address. After we have explored some of its major themes, I will highlight a few of the most familiar contemplations from the Exercises. In doing this my purpose is simply to indicate how relevant and generative the whole of the Spiritual Exercises can be for the life and mission of the Jesuit university today. Being rooted in the "school of the Exercises" keeps us in touch with the fundamental values and practices of our apostolic life and identity. If the university increases its prestige and its academic excellence, if it has grown its endowment and feels financially secure and is able to expand in whatever direction it chooses, if it achieves all these laudable and sensible aims that characterize every secular university, what has it gained if it has lost Christ and the grace of serving His mission?

A central feature of Jesuit life developed from the Spiritual Exercises is the "examen." Every Jesuit is personally formed in the daily reflective exercise, and our universities draw from it as well. The examen is not a limiting or rigid exercise; it is one that is as affective as it is cognitive, for it is about staying true to that which we love. It becomes a "habitus," a way of growing in the life of faith, seeking to stay faithful to the mission, judging what is essential from what is contingent.

Given that all institutions exercise their own centrifugal force, to what extent are we making the means (the institution) into an end? What are the subtle ways in which the commitment to the institution and its flourishing (a good) becomes a subtle way of providing a sense of security—apostolic, personal, and social—so that *we* become the ones who determine our own mission and set the criteria for its success?[8] These are the questions that an institutional discernment examen gives us: the freedom and the courage to ask about the reality of our institutional life. The challenge is to make our universities genuine communities of reflection. Without this we cease to be effective communities of learning.

The Transforming Perspective of Mission

Whether in the secular or spiritual field, mission entails a teleology that discloses identity and purpose. It must enter into every aspect of the university's life as a source of its creativity and self-transcendence. It provides an epistemological and hermeneutical frame for all its academic pursuits, its life as a community dedicated to research and learning as well as the formation of its members.

When we make this our epistemological ground and the creative source of imagination, we become the bearers of a hope that exposes the ephemeral nature of a future dependent on our own power and achievements.

Some Aspects of Discernment

If mission is the presupposition that runs through Jesuit life, there can be no effective mission without the exercise of discernment. This is made explicit at the opening of Father Sosa's address where he indicates that "preparing the future requires discerning the present." If universities are to respond to the needs of their students and contemporary society, they need to become communities of discernment, able to recognize the "signs of the times." This presupposes an openness to the Holy Spirit who is active in our lives, our institutions, and in history. It presupposes a fundamental trust that the Holy Spirit is at work even in the epistemological confusion and cacophony of voices that fill every culture, especially at moments of "deep story" change.[9]

Ignatius is not so much a speculative theologian as an experiential one. Out of his experience, he comes to know and recognize the God who is "laboring and working in all things" spoken of earlier as the salvific economy of grace. At first glance this may seem a rather obvious statement that fits into the scholastic principle that God is in all things by power, essence, and presence.[10] However, Ignatius does not present it as a theological proposition but as personal experience; the possibility of encounter in every situation of our existence. As such God is not only known as the Creator, first cause, or prime mover. God is known as both Creator and Redeemer which is a deeply personal encounter. The knowledge that flows from this abolishes a rather superficial oppositional division between sacred and secular on the one hand and challenges any illusion that God can be banished from the world on the other.

That God "labors and works in all things" is the liberative experience of divine action that requires a different approach to knowledge and understanding. It invites us to encounter God's salvific action in history, in the very dynamic of life itself. In this context, discernment is more than a matter of judgment; it is a personal (and communal) *attunement*—a "connaturality"—with the *way* in which God works, God's own "way of proceeding," developed through the praxis of Christian discipleship. It cannot be reduced to an analyzable formula to be replicated; it is always a free, gracious, and personal action that eludes our categories (cf. 1 Cor. 2:15–16).[11]

Discernment, then, requires us not just to "think" God in a procedural way. It must be lived, not instrumentalized. It demands that we enter into God's economy, not only at the level of our understanding but in the realities of our acting. Discernment presupposes such a relationship with God, and it is this relationship that constitutes the hermeneutical horizon for "reading the 'signs of the times' by discerning the present." If it is not this, then at best it can only be interpretations of the ambiguous contingencies already conditioned by our normal "situatedness." Discernment, however, is also "situated," but in a different way: It is a deliberate theological act that requires us to make a "preferential option for God," thereby placing "the times" and all they contain within the context of God's revelation. Discernment allows the divine light to illumine the present and disclose its significance within the history of salvation. In this regard, discernment is not some sort of esoteric knowledge or practice; it is part of the reality of all Christian life and discipleship. It will have a contemplative and a prophetic quality that opens the emerging uncertainties of the present to the horizon of God's action in Christ and the mission of the Holy Spirit. Discernment, then, can be seen as a coming to recognize and cooperate with God's way of acting, desiring the same good that God desires for all things, namely, participation and fulfilment in the triune life. Although beyond the scope of this essay to explore, what emerges here is the eschatological nature of discernment. If this is the horizon or the "end" with which discernment operates, it will then entail choices about the means appropriate to this end. The means will also draw from what we have learned about God's "way of proceeding" revealed in Christ. In this sense, discernment becomes a continuation and practice of our conversion to God.[12] Here we can see the intimate connection between discernment and the examen we have discussed. One of the fundamental challenges of the Ignatian perspective is the requirement that we move (conversion) from an anthropological centricity to one that is radically theocentric. Hence the essentially prophetic countercultural challenge intrinsic to the Society and its works.

In his address, Father Sosa expresses this in terms of a freedom to "let go of the reins," "to take risks," and the idea that "to discern is to be open to something new" (p. 11). Here, we meet the Gospel concept of *parrhesia*, which entails, but is more than, free and transparent speech. It is the capacity for bold and creative actions that open new possibilities for the Kingdom.[13] This can happen in the realms of thought and spirit as well as in concrete circumstances of our quotidian lives.

In the light of this brief discussion of mission and discernment it is clear that they are not a luxury or "value added" for the Jesuit university in a marketing campaign. Discernment becomes the principal way in which we possess the freedom in mission to "be guided towards something new."[14] If the discerning life of the university is rooted in the conviction that, like the Society, it is an instrument in God's hand, its theological orientation does not make discernment an exclusive religious activity only. Predicated on the immanent salvific work of God in all things, it requires an openness to all voices and traditions. In other words, mission creates an attentive and responsive space in which all can be heard and contribute according to their traditions, lights, and capacities.[15] The first work of discernment, then, must be an openness to the finite variety of God's action and a willingness to let our natural parochial horizons and prejudices be challenged. Paradoxically, the "theocentric situatedness" of discernment allows and requires the particularity of each historico-cultural "situatedness" to emerge; the distortions and limitations as well as those that are possibilities. It does not erase, silence, or disguise but calls into the light. This means that a discerning community will desire to be genuinely self-aware, open, reflective, and learning: one that is not afraid to confront itself and its own internal politics of power or the defensive silos of subjects and departments that can entrap and paralyze university communities.[16]

Discernment is an interior habit that becomes a culture and a way of life, institutional as well as personal. We cannot discern if we choose to live in a world where God is an afterthought or an occasional liturgical event. Notwithstanding all our mission statements and gestures toward the Jesuit ethos, we cannot discern if operationally we make our decisions and develop our strategic policies under the assumption that God does not exist.

If we want to create communities of reflection ordered to effective mission, we need to form all the members of our communities empowered to understand and participate in the processes of discernment. Each one will come with their own perspectives, questions, and suspicions. However, we are committed to help each to appreciate that their freedom is respected, not compromised or threatened, and that the habitus of discernment can become a source of life and creativity for all: "Discernment is knowing what is, in the light of what is possible from the perspective of God for whom nothing is impossible."[17] This is the charter of freedom that authentic discernment bestows.

Reflecting on Central Themes: The Unique Contribution of the Jesuit University

Out of the six themes in Father Sosa's address, I have chosen to reflect on two of them—first, "Persons with a Life of Full Meaning," and second, "A Mature Secularity." Important and fruitful though the other four are, I believe these two are central to understanding the particular culture of our universities and their mission.

Persons with a Life Full of Meaning

Father Sosa identifies a persistent, if subdued, crisis of meaning in our cultures. He notes three threats to our universities: fragmentation, superficiality, and instrumentality.[18] However, I think these threats are symptoms of a much deeper situation that faces our culture in general and is closely connected to the fifth theme of his address—"The University, Politics, Global Citizenship, Reconciliation and Peace," which argues that "through politics, meaning is given to social life."[19]

Here politics itself has a mission that can be obscured or distorted by the media and the precariousness of political systems. From the perspective of Catholic social thought, as David J. O'Brien explores in his contribution in this volume, politics is surely about the sustained attempt to realize the common good for all the members of society. If "the common good" is to be a stable reality, it must also extend to the international order. Whether domestic or international, a significant element entails finding those means that promote and sustain equality, reconciliation, justice, and "communion" between and within societies.[20] It is also urgent that we include the ecological dimension within the search for those means by which communion is sought.

As an accessible way to understand the dangers we are facing, Father Sosa draws on the work of Naim Moisés's *The Revenge of Power*. Moisés cogently argues that in the past democracy was threatened from without, but now it faces threats from within. He identifies "three 'Ps'": populism, polarization, and post-truth. These are operative internationally as well as at the level of domestic politics. The rise of authoritarian governments and populist leaders threatens to destabilize the international order. They learn from each other; they are adept at mobilizing and exploiting the latent anxieties of different groups within society. The autocrats and populists generate and utilize the identity crises that nations suffer when they feel "invaded" by migrants or "outsiders" are identified from within who are then portrayed as a threat to stability and prosperity. When nations or societies feel their foundational narratives are questioned and eroded, they can fall victim to the leader/messiah who can lead the nation back or forward to some mythical promised land, as evidenced in the slogan "Make America Great Again"—as if, somehow, America has lost something that needs to be recovered and secured. We can see the same sort of phenomenon play out in the Church's own "culture wars," as well as in secular society. In this context, the address invites universities to reflect on their role in promoting those values that sustain the political and social order, enabling the continued search for the common good and the restoration of substantive nonpolarizing social discourse, reflection, and debate.[21]

If the university is to be an authentic source of transformation, it must attend to agency. Here the reflection on freedom, discernment, and parrhesia ceases to be theoretical. The Jesuit university by virtue of its mission will attend not only to the intellectual formation of its students but to their moral and spiritual formation as well. If its education is to be truly and lastingly transformative, it will resist the instrumentalization of reason for a fuller, critical, and creative intellectual experience. It will be concerned with not only what knowledge is acquired but how that knowledge is employed.[22] This is why the Jesuit university, respecting the dignity of its students, will endeavor to give each one those resources that enable them to become authentic agents "because a democratic society seeks not only material prosperity but integral development that comes from pursuing the common good."[23] It will open the ways in which they can enter into the school of discernment and develop a freedom to recognize and resist the social, political, and economic forces of violence, division, exclusion, and exploitation that prevent the possibility of the common good. Jesuit education will aim to give each person the tools to recognize complicity and the ways in which we can become "implicated subjects," participants in erosion of democracy and its abuse.[24] The Church, too, faces similar threats to its discourse as does democracy, which also places its service of Truth at risk. The same qualities that are required for healthy participation in the social sphere are even more necessary in the ecclesial one.

While Moisés offers a clear and incisive description of the threats democracies face, I think the three Ps are symptoms of deeper questions than their causes. Human beings are in a constant search for meaning. If we cannot find secure meaning, we have to confront a fundamental, if unacknowledged, nihilism. The question of meaning cannot be separated from the question of the human person. It is the question that runs through the address: What type of person do we imagine as the fruit of the university experience that we propose?

Once more the search for meaning becomes critical at a personal and institutional level. It becomes especially urgent when the customary or traditional sources of meaning have been called into question. We should not ignore the fact that "meaning" is a complex reality, closely allied with our post-truth culture. Tutored by Friedrich Nietzsche and Michel Foucault, our culture has learned that truth is not the product of reason but of power. So the question becomes not "what is truth?" but rather "whose truth is it?" Equally, there is the cynical impatience of our hyper-culture that wants fast-food answers, "what is truth said jesting Pilate and would not stay for answer."[25]

Of course, in Foucault and Nietzsche the question itself is intended to serve a strategy of liberation. It is designed to unmask the oppressive hegemonies of our cultural narratives and those who control them. Even so, the critique creates its own culture—a culture of mistrust or suspicion that undermines faith in any "grand narrative" that generates meaning and provides continuity between generations and communities. If we are not careful, the strategy of "unmasking" becomes just as much a play for power as those that have been "unmasked." There is a dangerous situation in which the abandonment of reason rather than its liberation leads to social fragmentation and exploitation because power is unaccountable—a danger most evident in the rise of the digital world and its ambiguities—liberation, empowerment, escape?[26]

In this current phase of postmodernity, the "buffered self" and the "porous self" become the "anxious" or "fearful self." Meaning and identity are not grounded in any ontology as such but become constructed in the fluid and ephemeral forms of media and market and the unending search for security and "well-being." Meaning and existence become just the event-moments of a seemingly endless self-production and self-seduction, driven by the underlying anxiety and specter of the abyss or free fall into nothingness. Human historical consciousness is itself transformed even as it is globalized. In such a hyper-world, how can we find the relationships that sustain us and build the communities that value and nourish us? An existence whose only validation is the virtual is ipso facto without substance; it is a lonely place.[27]

From a Christian perspective, the "self," while having an ontological stability, also has a narrative dynamic: a person is in becoming through relationship. The person has a supernatural destiny; a life and an identity that is ordered to participation in the divine life. From this perspective, every human life has intrinsic value irrespective of ability, status, wealth, or "visibility." Indeed, as Christ demonstrates it is the socially "invisible" ones that God sees (Matt. 5.3–10). In our social settings the encounter with the divine perspective is both disruptive and prophetic precisely because it makes the invisible ones visible. Their presence cannot be denied or argued away. Christianity proves itself to be a "dangerous memory" in the social orders we construct; a threat to the systems of power that underpin them. Here, we encounter an important point for discernment. If our faith does not have this unsettling dimension but can only serve to legitimate a social order, then we must ask whose kingdom it serves.

In many ways, salvation is predicated not only on God's omnipotent love but on the radicalness of human freedom. For this reason, it cannot be separated from responsibility for ourselves and for others before God. It is in and through these relationships that we engaged in the narratives of our becoming. We learn through the experience and the wisdom of others, found in our great cultural traditions as well as in the lives of our friends and families, who teach us how to live with the incompleteness of our becoming, our fundamental inaccessibility to ourselves, our "enigma," until our history is fulfilled in God's presence (1 Cor. 12:13). They are part of our "making." We come to see that we live in the *poesis* that comes from the interplay of nature and grace (Eph. 2:4–10). It is a work, joyous and painful, but it is a coming into life.[28]

Who Do You Say That I Am?

Christ is also the epiphany of the human person called into life. The theocentric/Christocentric vision of the human person does not erase or diminish us. It reveals us in all our depth and dimensions of transcendence. Catholicism's theological anthropology is central to our identity as universities, and it constitutes the major contribution our educational apostolate makes to a society where the "human" and the meaning of "person" is contested.[29] However, as a reflective community it is important that we recognize our "operational anthropology." Our contemporary culture of suspicion will always be rightfully on the lookout for a disparity between what is said and what is done. In order to recognize and embed our understanding of the human person within all the activities of our lecture halls and communities, the examen becomes an essential practice of mission. How does our practice align with our rhetoric? Is it simply a gift-wrapped instrumentalization of the person as a consumer and potential wealth-generator (i.e., benefactor)? What are the success that we celebrate and the examples we promote? Is there a place for, and a recognition of, the *anawim* in our professional academic and student communities? In other words, how deep, how broad and how real, how humane is our actual vision of the human person?

The University: School of Humanity, School of Love, School of Encounter

"Being Christian is not the result of an ethical choice or a lofty idea, but the encounter with an event, a person, which gives life a new horizon and a decisive direction."[30] Jesuit universities are essentially schools of encounters from which meaning arises and expands in choices for the other. Father Sosa speaks clearly to the call to love in solidarity: "The substantive nucleus of human fulfilment is the love that becomes agape, that that is lived in common, gathering humanity around it."[31] More than anything else, it is love that nourishes us, body and soul. It is in love, and through love, that we experience the God who is Love.[32] It is through loving and through the works of love that we realize most completely our being made in God's own image, the essence of every person and their relationships.[33] It may not be the usual way in which we express the mission of the university, but surely it is integral to it. The Jesuit university strives to become a school of truth by which we come to love of God and love of neighbor.[34] This is the life that is full of meaning; it is the life that gives meaning to others. As a community that holds this vision of the person at its center, the university in all its activities contributes to forming persons who can do, speak, and live the truth in love.[35]

It can also do something more. The grace of a community that is committed to such a mission can also be a community of healing and acceptance, precisely because its center is Christ, who is the teacher of truth and love, forgiveness and reconciliation. Forgiveness and reconciliation for ourselves and for others are the new possibilities to which love introduces us. They teach us that we need not be locked in histories that we did not create. Forgiveness is the gratuitous exercise of our freedom. It cannot be compelled but it liberates us from the prisons of violence and prejudice. It is the gift we give to the future, that capacity for "natality," to begin anew, that Hannah Arendt takes from Augustine and holds it to be a uniquely human capacity. Forgiveness is its deepest form.

If love and the service of love fill a life with meaning and answer to our deepest questions of the self, our understanding would be incomplete without a brief word about suffering and solidarity.[36] There is nothing romantic about Christian love. At its heart there is always a realism, for God's love does not function as a talisman to deflect suffering but changes it. If anything, it calls for a solidarity with those who suffer; at its fullness it is about the transformation of suffering.[37] In Christ we see that the form of God's love is that of *kenosis*: a self-gift and self-emptying that secures a solidarity that deepens into union. Even though in the incarnation we see the kenosis of love at its most redemptive and profound, it is also part of our "ordinary" experience. In all our acts of parenting, friendship, teaching, and caring, wherever there is *cura personalis* and responsibility for the other, there is a *kenosis*.

Kenosis is generative. It is the relational energy of self-transcendence in self-gift that creates a deep communion, especially with and for those who suffer, in whom we see again Christ crucified. Especially today this must also entail solidarity with a crucified creation. In kenosis the heart is moved beyond empathy into compassion. In our freedom we choose to commit to the other in their suffering, even when they are our enemies. There is something here that we may not be fully aware of, but it is active within us by grace. We are always disposed to the other/Other. Even before we encounter them we are open to them, and this is grounded in our constitutive capacity for self-transcendence. It is not so much that they have made a claim on us, but we have committed ourselves to them in advance. Grounded in this depth, the Christian life can only be lived in a radical openness to the world; a love of all that is, guaranteed before any demand is made and given without any expectation of return.[38]

With such radical openness comes an understanding of our own vulnerability that is the necessary vulnerability entailed in every genuine openness to an encounter with the other. That vulnerability is constitutive of our person and is not a lack or a weakness so feared by contemporary culture and its Nietzschean theorists, but a graced openness is a new discovery.[39] This is the active solidarity and communion of Christian life that knows there is no "I" without "us" and seeks to realize this solidarity and communion as an active principle in all dimensions of our relations and social systems. Through this openness and commitment to the other, individually and institutionally, we can be sources of consolation and hope in a world "suffering for want of love" (Rom. 8:31–39).[40]

If the Jesuit university lives with a vision that cannot be caught by the normal metrics of success, nevertheless it can be experienced through the life of the community. In his address,

Father Sosa makes an important and, I think, critical observation. From its foundation the Society placed its emphasis on *"ayudar las almas"*: the help of souls. This was no mere conventional phrase; it embodied a vision of the human person, their intrinsic dignity and supernatural destiny. It opens a new horizon for our understanding. If part of the crisis of meaning is the reductivism with which our secular cultures view the human person, the Christian vision reminds us—against all reductivism— that the human person is soul as well as body. The soul, too, needs to be nourished if we are to flourish. One of the greatest obstacles to "persons with a life full of meaning" is the loss of interiority. The hunger for meaning cannot be satisfied without attention to the soul. Attention to this dimension of the person distinguishes the Jesuit university and its mission. The care of the whole person cannot be done without a love that seeks their lasting good and necessarily entails a concern for their eternal destiny. It is here, too, that the life of the community becomes important, for it is in the community that the whole person is also nurtured.

In all our interactions we model the society we wish to create. This becomes visible in the ways we choose to recognize difference, negotiate dissent, and reconcile conflict. Here, practice can be just as prophetic, and even more long-lasting in the lives of students, as the noble well-crafted statement. There is no shame, and certainly nothing to be feared, in acknowledging our own institutional failures and inadequacies. We know from our spirituality as well as our experience that there is no learning or progress in the intellectual, moral life or spiritual life without such honesty. In a society that lives in a crisis of trust our universities need to work to become communities of trust. Without this, "mission" is quickly reduced to sales talk and branding, "tinkling brass and sounding cymbals." How we model and perform the freedom that our mission gives becomes the touchstone of our integrity.

Where deep learning is taking place, results are not always immediately apparent. It is often the enduring examples of commitment, effort, and perseverance that measure fidelity to the vision. It is these qualities, too, that establish a history and tradition. They give substance to what is said and lived that can be trusted because it has been proved over time. Every institution lives in time through those who are witnesses to the values it seeks to instill and celebrate. As we know from the testimonies of those who have long since graduated, it is these unseen values, glimpsed in the example of colleagues, students and alumni which continue to sustain our professional and personal lives. Their witness and example protect the truth that inspires us. In the daily fidelities to values, vision, and routines that make up the ordinary life of every institution we discover that, invisible and unprogrammed, it is our relationships that become the channels of grace. When the bright colors of honors have faded, and the cheers of graduation have become a distant echo, our relationships can continue to bear fruit. We live and work through faith, servants of the mystery unfolding in the lives of students and staff and only grasped in part. The work of all education is perfected in the patient fidelity to the mission we have received and faith in the Lord who gives it.

A Mature Secularity

In the section of his address on "Sowing in Thirsty Soil," Father Sosa speaks a "mature secularity" that is not an enemy to our faith or mission but is for us the "vineyard of the Lord."[41] A mature secularity also requires a mature catholicity: a faith that can see God laboring and working even in those places where God is denied, forgotten, or confined to the private closet of personal taste. A university whose epistemology and hermeneutics of the secular is informed by the Spiritual Exercises—particularly by Ignatius's vision of "God laboring and working in all things"—will know that the secular cannot be a barrier to God, nor can God be banished from our world or its history. Our mission, therefore, is not to overcome the secular but to enable it to mature.

Such a commitment of service begins by recognizing that "the secular" is itself in crisis. Although secular modernity has its own prophets who can point to scientific progress, we cannot ignore the precariousness of the consensus that underpins the notion of human rights or the daily atrocities that humanity commits. Augustine was not a pessimist but a realist when it came to recognizing the dynamics of human desire, the quest for power, and the capacity for moral self-delusion. The work of helping to bring about a mature secularity will thus seek to generate relationships that "permit the exercise of human freedom in the different dimensions of life, opening spaces for human creation."[42] It will not lose sight of the capacity of humanity for the good; it will seek to find those structures and systems that can command the trust of all the people whom they are authorized to serve. It will seek to construct those systems that embody values that can inspire and encourage the always unfinished moral and spiritual work that any good society requires.

A mature secularity will not exclude the need of grace—in whatever form it manifests itself—or see it as a threat. It will understand that the principle "grace does not obliterate nature but perfects it" applies to social structures as well as persons. When this occurs we can see the true enlightenment of the secular.

A mature secularity is also a grace for the necessary renewal of the pilgrim Church in via. A liberated vision of the secular requires that Catholicity too is open to the reciprocity that such a relationship entails. Through our engagement with a mature secularity and openness to its critique, our Catholic culture also grows. True, we may have to accept that to serve the secular well, we have to endure misunderstanding and even forms of persecution. Yet whatever the circumstances in which we find ourselves, our faith does not absolve us from a patient, committed generosity necessary for bringing about the lasting human good and the structures that express it.[43]

The Sources for a Mature Secularity

A mature secular society must experience its own "thirst." A confident democracy will be open to the other sources on which it draws, and that remain beyond its immediate control. The Böckenförde Dilemma articulates this well: "The liberal secular state lives on premises that it cannot itself guarantee."[44] As well as "other sources of the self," Böckenförde acknowledges the significance of religion as a key dimension in the life of the secular state. To put it theologically, every society must come to acknowledge how it lives from gifts (graces) that it cannot create and are beyond its ultimate control. It relies not only on the gifts of nature but on those human gifts that cannot be coerced or manipulated through false promises and illusory offers. Where such attempts at coercion or manufacturing self-confirming and nurturing resources take place, society ultimately degrades and contaminates the very soil in which it lives. It leaves only a desert of exploitation and suppression, in which persons are devalued. Such societies will always find the Christian truth a threat.

The Church, however, is not a "resident alien" in a secular society, even though it may be treated as such. Under penalty of betraying its own mission, it must not succumb to accepting exile as the premise of its existence. No matter how scarred humanity is by the effects of its fallenness or burdened by the great weight of so much unresolved suffering and broken dreams, the Church that is founded on the death and resurrection of Jesus Christ cannot be anywhere else but in this world and its history. Indeed, it is because of these very things that the Church is sent into the world, a source of its healing and its hope. Even with its own flawed history, the remains through the gracious dispensation of God's faithfulness, the universal sacrament of salvation. The Church shares in the kenosis of her Lord.[45] It must be part of the mission of our universities to cultivate faith in the Church, to draw from her deep traditions and witness to nourish the present and resource the future. It means understanding that the Church can never be confused by the world, but this very distinction is precisely so that it can relate more deeply to it and serve it in freedom.

In a world of fragile democracies and growing authoritarian regimes, where truth is defined by power rather than critical debate and reason, the task of the Church is to offer an emancipatory re-narration through which societies can discover new, liberating possibilities and restorative praxis: "Through her work, whatever good is in the minds and hearts of men [*sic*], whatever good lies latent in the religious practices and cultures of diverse peoples, is not only saved from destruction but is also cleansed, raised up, and perfected unto the glory of God, the confusion of the devil and the happiness of man."[46]

The way in which our universities can serve the commitment of the Church to a "mature secularity" is to form people intellectually with a generosity of thought, to help them grow in the freedom of discernment and the service of others, with the courage to resist destructive, instrumental, and abusive power, to have the courage to "live in the truth"; to be builders of peace founded on justice, creative witnesses of forgiveness and reconciliation. In short, in whatever path or creed they choose, to be disciples of the life of Kingdom. This will require perseverance and communities that are deeper and richer than alumni associations, committed to the educational and cultural mission of our universities, working in hope that they can and do make a difference until His Kingdom comes.[47]

Notes

1. Constitutions §813.
2. Cf. Apple website. The Newsroom presents Apple as a major contributor to the common good with its products and its support for values and projects.
3. Cf. GC 34. d.2: "'Servants of Christ's Mission," especially the emphasis on the mission of the Risen Christ and the graces that Christ gives, §32–38. Also, GC 35. d.2, §14.
4. Cf. The Formula of the Institute, *The Constitutions of the Society of Jesus and Their Complementary Norms: A Complete English*

Translation of the Official Latin Texts (St. Louis: Institute of Jesuit Sources, 1996 [series 1, no. 15]), 3–16.

5. Cf. GC 35 d.2. §11–13. As Bernard Lonergan argues, the law of the cross is a "law" that brings transformation, following Rom. 12. 21, the self-sacrificing love that brings good out of evil. Cf. Bernard J. F. Lonergan, *Collected Works of Bernard Lonergan: The Redemption*, ed. Robert M. Doran, et al. Trans. Michael G. Shields (Toronto: University of Toronto Press, 2018), 203ff. See esp. Part 5, Thesis 17.

6. Sp. Exx. §136–147.

7. The phrase occurs a number of times in the Constitutions, §64, 66, 70–71, 136, 211, 238, 343, 351, 382, 455 and 746. The phrase itself indicates the adaptability requires of the missionary Society and the capacity to discern so that the essential identity and character is also preserved while other factors are considered.

8. Cf. The Three Classes of Men, Sp. Exx. § 149.

9. The concept of "deep story" is developed by the sociologist Arlie Russell Hochschild in her *Strangers in Their Own Land: Anger and Mourning on the American Right* (New York: Free Press, 2016). The Spiritual Exercises also attend to the deep story and relocate it in the deeper story of God's salvific love in Christ.

10. This formulation also occurs in the Sp. Exx §39.2, but it is concerned with the question of swearing by the name of God. The formula is treated by Aquinas in demonstrating God's omnipresence ST.1.8, art. 1–4.

11. "Dios trabaja y labora por mi en todas cosas criadas sobre la haz la terra . . .": Sp. Exx. §236 summarises this experiential knowledge which is echoed throughout the Exercises. It is also important to recognise that, for Ignatius, "discreta caritas" is part of the discernment which is tied to "busar y hallar la vuluntad de Dios" and "amando y sirviendo en todo . . ." (Sp. Exx. §233). For a critical review of the Jesuit influence on how we think about discernment and the influence of the Jesuit-edited *Dictionnaire de spiritualité*, cf. Kees Waaijman, "Discernment and Biblical Spirituality: An Overview and Evaluation of Recent Research," *Acta Theologica*, Supplement 7 (2013): 1–12.

12. For this reason we must distinguish discernment from the virtue of prudence, although it does not exclude it.

13. For the biblical tradition, cf. R. W. L. Moberly, *Prophecy and Discernment* (Cambridge, UK: Cambridge University Press, 2006). Also useful is P. De Villiers, P. B. Decock, and K. Waaijman, *The Spirit That Guides: Discernment in the Bible and Spirituality* (Bloemfontein, South Africa: University of the Free State, 2013), Acta Theologica Supplementum: 17.

14. RPG Address, 2.
15. Op. cit., 2.
16. It is useful to read the General's IAJCU Address address with his recent book *Walking with Ignatius: In Conversation with Darío Menor* (Dublin: Messenger Publications, 2021), esp. 230–231 on the necessary plurality of the university.
17. Richard of St. Victor, cited in Kees Waaijman, "Discernment and Biblical Spirituality: An Overview and Evaluation of Recent Research," *Acta Theologica*, Supplement 7 (2013): 1–12; 9.
18. As well as the impact of fragmentation of culture through various forms of relativism, Alasdair MacIntyre traces the challenges facing universities back to the nature of modernity and the compartmentalization of knowledge. Cf. Alasdair MacIntyre, "Catholic Universities: Dangers, Hopes, Choices," in *Higher Learning and Catholic Traditions*, ed. Robert E. Sullivan (Notre Dame, IN: University of Notre Dame Press, 2001).
19. RPG, 8.
20. Pope Francis, *Encyclical Letter: Fratelli Tutti of the Holy Father Francis on Fraternity and Social Friendship* (London: Catholic Truth Society, 2020). Cf. Suzanne Mulligan, ""Builders of a New Social Bond": Fratelli Tutti on Good Politics and the Challenge of Inequality," *The American Journal of Economics and Sociology* 80, no. 4 (2021): 1173–1203.
21. For a succinct critique of political discourse, cf. *Fratelli Tutti*, chapter 5. In this, the initiative of the USCCB "Civilize It. Dignity Beyond Debate" remains a good example; cf. http://www.civilizeit.org
22. The question at the center of Mary Fulbrook, *Bystander Society: Conformity and Complicity in Nazi Germany and the Holocaust*, (Oxford, UK: Oxford University Press. 2023).
23. RPG, 8. In this respect the dynamic of the Two Standards is formative and transformative. Sp. Exx. §136–148.
24. Cf. Michael Rothberg, *The Implicated Subject: Beyond Victims and Perpetrators* (Stanford, CA: Stanford University Press, 2019).
25. Francis Bacon, "Essay on Truth" (1597).
26. Jamie Susskind, *The Digital Republic: Taking Back Control of Technology* (London: Bloomsbury Publishing, 2023); also important is Susskind's wider argument that a "republic" is or should be designed to oppose any one group holding unaccountable power.
27. Noreena Hertz, *The Lonely Century: How to Restore Human Connection in a World That's Pulling Apart* (New York: Currency, 2021).
28. Cf. Amos N. Wilder, the New Testament scholar and poet's conviction that "the real impasse of the Gospel today is to be found at the

point of the deed rather than languages and images" (introduction to *Grace Confounding* [Eugene, OR: Wipf and Stock, 1972]: x).

29. For an overview of a Christian anthropology that informs a Catholic humanist tradition to which Jesuit universities are committed, cf. *Gaudium et Spes*, chapters I–III.

30. Deus Caritas Est §1.

31. RPG, 4.

32. Augustine, "Amplectere dilectionem Deum et dilectione amplectere Deum." De. Trinitate. Bk 8.12.

33. Cf. James Hanvey, SJ, "Dignity, Person and Imago Trinitatis," in *Understanding Human Dignity*, ed. C. McCrudden (Oxford, UK: Oxford University Press, 2013), Proceedings of the British Academy; 192: 209–28.

34. Mater et Magistra §226ff.

35. Eph. 4:15. The Vulgate gives, "veritatem autem facientes in caritate crescamus in illo per omnia qui est caput Christus." The usual translation is "speaking the truth in love we are to grow in all aspects into Him who is the head, that is, Christ." Both are appropriate in this context.

36. RPG, 10. F: With and for others.

37. Cf. especially Michael Gorman's important study *Inhabiting the Cruciform God: Kenosis, Justification, and Theosis in Paul's Narrative Soteriology* (Grand Rapids, MI: Eerdmans, 2009).

38. Cf. Sp. Exx. §230–237; Pope Benedict XVI, Spe Salvi, §39. I am suggesting that for the human to be created in the image and likeness of God must mean not only that human nature has an openness to the divine (deification or theosis) but an openness to all created things. There is an inescapable moral dimension to our being persons. "Love of neighbor" is not only a moral injunction but an ontological law of our becoming that stands with love of God. Vladimir Lossky, *Dogmatic Theology* (Yonkers, NY: St. Vladimir's Seminary Press, 2017), 85–88.

39. Cf. Enda McDonagh, *Vulnerable to the Holy in Faith, Morality and Art* (Dublin: Columba, 2004); Erinn C. Gilson, *The Ethics of Vulnerability: A Feminist Analysis of Social Life and Practice* (Oxfordshire, UK: Routledge, 2014); James F. Keenan, "The World at Risk: Vulnerability, Precarity, and Connectedness," *Theological Studies (Baltimore)* 81, no. 1 (2020): 132–49.

40. The intimate connection between love and kenosis is explored philosophically in the phenomenologies of Jean-Luc Marion, *Prolégomènes à la charité*, rev. and expanded ed. (Paris: Bernard Grasset, 2018) and Jean-Luc Marion and S. E. Lewis, *The Erotic Phenomenon*

(Chicago: University of Chicago Press, 2007); also, Jean-Luc Marion and S. E. Lewis, *Being Given: Toward a Phenomenology of Givenness* (Stanford, CA: Stanford University Press, 2002); and Jean-Louis Chrétien, *Le regard de l'amour* (Paris: Desclée de Brouwer, 2000).

41. RPG, 5.

42. RPG, 5.

43. Cf. *Gaudium et Spes, esp.* Chapter 4. Also Ormond Rush, *The Vision of Vatican II: Its Fundamental Principles* (Collegeville, MN: Liturgical Press Academic, 2019), esp., 480ff.

44. Articulated by Ernst-Wolfgang Böckenförde, a German legal scholar and political philosopher, cf. "The Rise of the State as a Process of Secularization [1967]," in Mirjam Künkler and Tine Stein (eds.), *Religion, Law, and Democracy: Selected Writings*, trans. Thomas Dunlap (Oxford, UK: Oxford University Press, 2020), 154–167. Part of Böckenförde's thesis is that society can only survive if its civil liberties receive support from its citizens, but it cannot produce this by law or force without destroying its own legitimacy and foundations. For a more complete discussion, cf. Bryan S. Turner, "Secular and Religious Citizenship" in *The Oxford Handbook of Citizenship* (Oxford, UK: Oxford University Press, 2017), 489ff. See also the debate between Jürgen Habermas and Cardinal Joseph Ratzinger, *Dialektik der Säkularisierung* (Freiburg: Herder, 2005).

45. Cf. *Gaudium et Spes* §1–3; also Chapter 4, which sets out this commitment to the world. Cf. also H. U. von Balthasar, who emphasizes the Christological form of kenosis in its Marian and institutional implications: "The Kenosis of the Church?" in *Explorations in Theology*, Vol. IV (San Francisco, CA: Ignatius Press, 1995), 125–38.

46. *Lumen Gentium* §17. Cf. also James Hanvey SJ, "The Challenge and Hope of *Gaudium et Spes*," in *The Church in the Modern World: Fifty Years After Gaudium et Spes*, ed. E. Brigham (Lanham, MD: Lexington Books, 2015), esp. 16–30.

47. The Catholic—and especially the Jesuit—university has a critical role in helping the Church realize its mission in the world by equipping its members to fulfil their vocation. Cf. Vatican II, *Apostolicam Actuositatem* and Chapter 5 of *Lumen Gentium*.

4

Reconciliation and Jesuit Higher Education

Embracing Our Shared Work as Spiritual Gift and Social Task

Gordon Rixon, SJ

Introduction: The Transcendent Promise of Reconciliation

IN MARCH 2023, THE SOCIETY of Jesus in Canada released a list of Jesuits who had been credibly accused of the sexual abuse of a minor in the previous fifty years. The next day, I was walking across the University of Toronto campus from the Regis College, the Jesuit School of Theology, where I serve as president, to a sister institution at the university. While the sister institution is a small residential college, it is also a renowned international focal point for academic and social exchange. I was to join prominent civil and Indigenous leaders, scholars, and Knowledge Keepers to offer remarks as we installed an Eagle Feather gifted by a past national Indigenous leader in the college's chapel. Without suggesting readers should fully appreciate the specific social roles, cultural prestige, and public voice assembled by the occasion and associated with the place, I simply ask benevolent readers to grant that my apprehension that things could soon go very badly was well grounded.

Somewhere in the verdant park that separates Regis from the central spine of the campus, my apprehension became focused as I set my mind on what seemed the only available course of action. As I entered the college quadrangle and approached the chapel, my intended plan of action was aided by the presence of a small group of Knowledge Keepers standing by the chapel entrance waiting for the arrival of the platform party. Addressing the group, "Is it ok," I asked, "for me to be here today?" "I was abused by a Catholic priest but not a Jesuit," responded a surprisingly friendly voice with just a touch of dark humor. "Of course, you are welcome."

Somehow, in that moment, something gifted from beyond myself and my companions held the generative contention of truth-telling, vulnerability, mutual acknowledgment, the demand for justice, resilience, courage, and the promise of more profound solidarity.

My reflections here begin with two theological observations grounded in this gift. First, we do not save ourselves. Second, God does not save us without us. Reconciliation, in sum, is a spiritual gift and a social task, an undomesticated, transcendent contention that eludes control and resolution as it charges the social field in which Jesuit higher education and other contemporary social and cultural institutions draw their breath and speak their truths. Reconciliation is a historical dynamic understood by the Christian as the interplay between the two missions of Spirit and Word unfolding in the world.

Secularity, Ambiguity, Pluralism: Keys to Understanding Our Current Context

Before we probe the spiritual and theological resources afforded by the expression of these two divine missions, some preliminary reflections must clear a space for engaging the role of religion in higher education institutions sponsored by faith communities operating in secularized social sectors and culturally fragmented societies. Truth-telling about clerical sexual abuse and the role of the Roman Catholic and other Christian communities in genocidal colonization threatens to debase institutional self-esteem and identity and delegitimate the public voice of Jesuit and other religiously sponsored schools. Consequently, three remarks are in order.

First, as Father Sosa's address suggests, secularism is not necessarily a negative phenomenon that needs to be reversed. There is a mature secularism that throws aside oppressive clericalism, state-funded and aligned churches, and other overreaching distortions of religion without denigrating or impeding the higher, self-transcending aspirations of human living. As the Canadian Jesuit philosopher and theologian Bernard Lonergan remarked, there are distinct secularisms to be avoided and promoted.[1] Aggressive secularism can vilify religion as an enemy to be eliminated and deliberately or unwittingly reduce the self-transcending scope of human aspiration. The "thirsty ground" of the mature secularism envisioned by Sosa creates a positive climate of freedom that advances faith practice unshackled from the imposition of established religion and self-promoting religious leaders and practitioners.[2]

No less, Lonergan maintains, there are sacralizations to be avoided and to be promoted. Some forms of sacralization arise from enervating superstitions and alienated human agency and become the prestige-distorted instruments of social privilege and control. In *A Secular Age*, Charles Taylor analyzes the porous, nonbuffered self subject to the providential and demonic spirit forces of an enchanted universe and privileged social orders claiming the legitimation of divine or hereditary ordination.[3] Yet finding the self-transcending spiritual dimension of daily life can foster life-giving sacralizations that raise the focus of human desire and creative activity to parcicipate freely in a higher, divine purpose.

Lonergan's crosscutting analysis of secularization and sacralization allows us to reframe the culture war imbroglio and illustrates the constructive potential of learned faith-based civic engagement. Would not mature secularism and the desire for self-transcending sacralization join in calling out the false sacral-ization of consumerism? Are humans destined to function as homogenized consumers of standardized mass production? Might not a more mature and adequate understanding and re-spect for natural, social, and cultural ecologies seek the purpose and meaning of the everyday, ever mindful of self-serving misap-propriations of the sacred?[4]

A second preliminary reflection acknowledges religious practice's ambiguity in differentiating religion's sociological and transcendent functions. Religion is and always has been am-biguous. The scandal of clergy sexual abuse and the association of the Church with the genocidal residential school system pro-vide ample historical evidence. Sometimes we take the idea of enclosure as an architectural feature of monasteries and a liter-ary device in religious writings much too literally. While enclo-sure as a trope sets the Church apart from the world as an idealized society, a moment's reflection assures us that good and evil exist in the world, in the Church, in faith communi-ties, and in the self. The challenge is to adopt a self-critical stance, resolve less than fully conscious tendencies, and allow continuous discernment to correct our perceptions and guide our actions.

The notion of enclosure draws our attention to another reality that shares this ambiguity more subtly, which touches on identity and belonging. We must distinguish religion's sociological and transcendent functions to sort out this ambiguity. Religion's socio-logical function creates and maintains group cohesion. The an-thropologist Robin Dunbar investigated the correlation between social group size and group cohesion maintenance strategies in primates and humans.[5] Primates can maintain a cohesive troop size of about forty-five through fingertip grooming. With ad-vanced cognitive skills, humans can develop more sophisticated approaches—choral singing and Christmas card lists are exam-ples. Singing enables sympathetic breathing, which is a very effec-tive bonding practice. Christmas card lists usually peak at about 150 entries. Binding people together through sharing meanings and values is a more expansive strategy, which religion can implement broadly and effectively. As a group cohesion strategy, however, religion can bind people together or drive them apart. Religion can be a creative instrument of peacemaking and reconciliation or incite sectarian violence.[6] Enclosure can signal welcoming hospitality enriched by a lively self-reflective interculturality or be a cruel instrument of social exclusion.[7]

Religion's transcendence function invites us to recognize and serve a divine purpose higher than group cohesion. While religion legitimately recognizes our profoundly social nature, its purpose goes beyond the security of belonging to a social group dedicated to the praise, reverence, and service of the creator God. Even as the transcendent function affirms the right to culture, the dignity of social identity, and the importance of belonging to a tradition of meanings and values, its divine purpose remains beyond the grasp of any culture, identity, or tradition.[8] While the transcendent function affirms and promotes religion's sociological function, higher purpose cannot be instrumentalized in the interest of group cohesion without undermining its life-enhancing integrity.

Truth-telling in a post-truth world must overcome obfuscation to acknowledge the malfeasance of clergy sexual abuse, racism, and the tepidity of contemporary institutional responses. These systemic failures have discredited religious institutions and leadership and brought religion's sociological function into critical relief.[9] The sociological and transcendent functions have starkly separated in the contemporary Western imagination. The two no longer coincide in a compact notion of religion.

In many Western countries the practice of personal spirituality appears to overshadow the transcendent function of religion. Religion has become associated predominantly with the ambiguous sociological function of group cohesion. Widespread social perception identifies religious leadership and adherence with promoting exclusionary social identity, social privilege, self-protection, and even sectarian violence. The transcendent function endures in spiritual practices loosely affiliated or totally unaffiliated with traditional faith communities.

While distinguishing religion's transcendent and sociological functions promises to subject religious practice and authority to appropriate public scrutiny and accountability, disengaging personal spirituality from communal religious practice neglects the social aspects of human and spiritual formation. The sociological function of religion remains as inevitable and necessary as it is de facto ambiguous. Differentiating and reintegrating religion's social and transcendent functions requires cultivating reflective spiritual and critical intellectual practices to identify, discern, and reshape attitudes and actions flowing from otherwise less-self-aware group identification. Moving beyond the tendency of the contemporary narrative about personal spirituality to eclipse the constructive social role of religion, a renewal of religious practice, leadership, and institutions requires spiritual and intellectual formation accompanied by a critical understanding of the dynamics of social belonging.

A final preliminary reflection locates the challenge of social belonging in an evolving context of attitudes toward pluralism. Immediately after the Second Vatican Council, Roman Catholics struggled to integrate change into their spiritual lives. Seemingly fixed religious practices and rituals began to change, sometimes weekly. Solidly set altars moved. Liturgies adopted the vernacular. Scriptural study and new theological methodologies emerged. Clergy lost their exclusive claim to religious leadership and an exemplary lifestyle. Church documents asked all the baptized to adopt the goal of holiness and active participation in their faith communities.[10] Rapid social change soon spread to every sector of society.

New cohorts of young people, including those training for church ministry, were so immersed in change that many lost a sense of participating in a historical project. Their lives and experience of the sacred became a series of disconnected episodes. For them, theology is disassociated from its historical context not because it is eternal but because historical movements have lost their substance and direction. These youth struggled to engage in a divine project because conceiving and committing to a divine venture expressed in a historical movement eluded their grasp. Such a venture would require the widely discredited possibility of a "metanarrative." Amid this social turmoil, cohorts of so-called young conservatives reframed their challenge as resisting moral relativism and focused on recovering a fixed moral compass. Pluralism became the opponent.[11]

Today, many of those engaged in theological formation seem to dwell at ease within a new world shaped by historical consciousness and proactive interculturality. Ideally, if not typically, this ease signals possession of the gifts of self-critical cultural awareness. Pluralism per se is no longer perceived as a sparring partner but is acknowledged prima facie as an expression of the generous bounty of divine goodness and beauty. Truth is symphonic, and its fuller expression requires time to engage the affordances of the world's many languages and cultures.[12] While individual sin and social injustice also take pluriform root in diverse languages and cultural meanings and values, the primary agents of discernment and reform are those intimately embedded in these manifold contexts.[13] In each instance, the Christian believes the redeeming light of the Paschal Mystery overcomes populism, polarization, and post-truth to bring fuller expressions of the faithful, salving divine justice that is mercy.

For this recent cohort, their struggle is not recognizing pluralism as a gift but addressing the existential questions Where do I belong? How do I participate? Without arguing that any of these cohorts are ultimately more than ideal types offering some structure for understanding threads of our recent history, those aligning with this final cohort have reframed their situation most transparently in the human condition. There is something attractive about the honesty of their acknowledgment of vulnerability and interdependence. Their achievement lies less in the answer to the presenting questions as the way of identifying and holding the challenge.

Encounter, Dialogue, and Spiritual Conversation: The Journey Toward Reconciliation

The contention of secularism, pluralism, and belonging in individual lives and the historical movements of communities provides the context for theological reflection on journeys toward reconciliation. Some aggrieved communities take exception to the notion of "reconciliation," observing that there was no original conciliation to be restored. This charge has been put forth, for instance, by several Indigenous communities who have suffered the denigration of their culture, language, and land-based economic activity through colonization.[14] During Pope Francis's July 2022 penitential pilgrimage with Indigenous communities across Canada, he reflected on the meaning of conciliation as bringing issues to council to be addressed by an assembly of those concerned.[15] This process of encounter and dialogue signals a pivotal practical shift in the approach of the highest level of leadership in the Roman Catholic Church. This transformation is finding further expression in the process adopted by the Synod on Synods, unfolding in two sessions after extended preparation in local dioceses and continental regions.

In the first session of the Synod, which concluded in November 2023, Pope Francis and those planning the synodal program (re)introduced the Church to spiritual conversation.[16] As an iterative process of prayer, reflection, and structured exchange, this experientially based shared reflection is as ancient and contemporary as practicing faith communities. Such faith-informed dialogue invites profound transformation of individual and shared practice of the faith that brings to light and eclipses ideologies and political positioning. While the description of spiritual conversation sounds simple and its practice is straightforward, the pursuit and fruits of spiritual conversation depart dramatically from the common polarizing civil discourse that characterizes public exchange today. To appreciate the quiet revolution that Francis is advancing, we might consider spiritual conversation in its most basic form in small group settings and then highlight its significance for larger faith communities and the universal Church and their engagement in civil society.

In its contemporary small group form, spiritual conversation can be a three-moment process. The first moment could involve a short period of quiet, reflective prayer and an initial round of sharing. During this time, participants notice their interior, spiritual responses to a prompt, such as recalling times of encouragement, joy, sadness, and discouragement in the past month. Participants could ask themselves: When have I felt drawn into a closer union with Christ, family, friends, and coworkers? When have I felt isolated from Christ and those with whom I live and work? Were there tepid moments when I was drifting away from a closer union? Moments associated, for instance, with soft addictions such as extended periods of passive media consumption. Were there difficult periods when I was moving into closer union? Moments related, for example, to the cost of accompanying and advocating for those who suffer racism, homophobia, or other forms of social exclusion. What interior or exterior events triggered shifts in the direction of my spiritual movements? Perhaps overlooked events sparked the development of dispositions of gratitude and generosity or self-promotion and self-protection? Then, after considering my interior movements further, I share some representative events and interior responses that respect others and build trust in the group.

The actual sharing is brief and structured by a generous spirit of attentive, respectful listening without immediate discussion or challenge. After holding what others contribute for a few moments of further reflection, the process's second moment involves a second round of sharing. Here, the invitation is to notice the spiritual movement in the present moment. How is the group being moved here and now? Where do I see a movement to union with Christ in the sharing? Cultivating heightened and immediate self-awareness takes time, practice, and a willingness to make, notice, and learn from mistakes. The invaluable fruit is a gathering of reflective data and a growing capacity to continue conversations in the process's third moment that nurtures the intellectual flexibility, affective freedom, and thoughtful discernment required to walk with others in the service of a divine project beyond the definitive grasp of any single participant.

A Synodal Church in Mission, the synthesis report of the 2023 Synod, affirms that the Church does not *have* a mission but *is* a mission. In doing so, the text flags the similar challenge of reducing the distance between intimate spiritual experience and the stories we tell about such religious experience.[17] This enigmatic phrase—does not *have* a mission but *is* a mission—introduces the creative contention of Spirit and Word, a contention in which we participate and that we imitate.[18] The Spirit is the very life force, the breath we received as gift. A gift given to us without conditions or reservations that draws us continuously into an enduring relationship over which we do not exercise control. First quietly dwelling in us as the love of God by which we love God and then voiced actively at Pentecost in the evangelical charge to share the Gospel of peace, justice, and hope. The Word shapes the gift of divine breath in the events of history—first quietly expressed in the act of creation and then voiced eloquently in the redeeming mystery of Christ's passion, death, and resurrection. In these generative oppositions, tensive distinctions in unity, we remain a mystery to ourselves unfolding in history as we discover the source of our being and the reach of our spiritual desire.[19]

For us, a fuller resonance between Spirit and Word—interior movement and self-disclosure, in dialogue and action cultivated in spiritual conversation—is a constant aspiration. Our lives are a pilgrimage—sometimes penitential as we acknowledge evident shortcomings, sometimes searching for a God still unknown, sometimes savoring the intimacy of interior movements at the dusk of day.[20] Only in the life of Christ do we see a perfect, harmonic resonance between the gift of breath and its eloquent expression in history.

In the synodal process, Pope Francis reminds us that we do not travel the path alone. The first session in October 2023 was a gathering of those who journey together, an admonishment not to leave companions to the side, and an invitation to listen carefully to the voicing of the Spirit and Word in the biographies of individuals and the histories of cultures and peoples. The second session held in October 2024 drew our discerning attention to the immediacy and urgency of our desire and the invitation to serve a world in need of hope.

The Examen, Discernment, and the Work of Trauma Recovery: An Ignatian Approach to Social Reconciliation

Father Sosa appeals to the evolving Jesuit understanding of "for and with others" as he invites Jesuit institutions of higher learning to embrace a similar synodal culture of intercultural and intergenerational dialogue in the service of social reconciliation.[21] Pursuing this end, the spiritual gifts cultivated by the Ignatian Spiritual Exercises and the insights of the human sciences advise each other and lead us to deepen self-awareness and self-critical practice. Developing such deliberate agency and creative practice requires self-knowledge and psychological freedom. The Exercises curate this interior development. Critical human sciences refine our self-knowledge and suggest how we could engage in the project of living well together. Theology guides and offers corrective suggestions about the mutual mediation of spirituality and the human sciences. Jesuit colleges and universities are charged with creating the space for this three-cornered conversation. An illustrative example is the mutual mediation of the Ignatian examen and psychological insight into the trauma recovery process under the illumination of a theological appreciation of the Paschal Mystery. We discuss this example in three steps. We describe the damaging impact of trauma on human identity and agency. We then compare the trauma recovery process with the five steps of the examen. Finally, we flag the significance of holding a trauma-informed account of the examen under the light of the Paschal Mystery and valorizing redeemed agency and the "reremembering" of the journey toward restorative justice.

Understood in the context of social anthropology, trauma is the product of an overwhelming violent or other negative experience that undermines relationships with others, ourselves, and even our own bodies.[22] Our identities, agency, and capacity to respond to threats are profoundly compromised by trauma. Self-confidence, self-respect, and self-esteem are disrupted.[23] Our fight, flight, freeze, and fawn responses to threats become disconnected from our immediate situation. We struggle to control hypervigilant reactions and may withdraw from the sensory stimulations of typical daily life. We lose our ability to maintain a buffer between sensory stimulation and the identity-affirming stories we tell about ourselves. We can no longer distinguish between self and the tsunamis of sensory experiences that inundate the self.

Trauma theory suggests three moments provide direction to the path to recovery. First, the traumatized person needs to retrieve a basic sense of safety. This retrieval is often fragile and achieved incrementally and lost iteratively. The first steps in this phase of the recovery journey typically require the active assistance of a compassionate caregiver. In the second moment, the active caregiver must transform into an encouraging witness as persons in recovery begin to reactivate their agency through narration and valorization. They tell a story in their own terms about what happened and reassert the values that were harmed. The very telling of the story and the assertion of the values begin to restore their compromised agency and recreate the buffer between the self and the harmful experience. The wise caregiver adopts a passive role so as not to impede the person in recovery's reemerging agency.

The final and continuing moment is a progressive movement to overcome self-isolation and repair damaged social relations. This moment may yield social activism confronting the injustice and other remediable issues associated with the previous traumatizing harm. Reemerging agency is expressed and reinforced through expanding collaboration, shared values, and joint action.

I want to propose that the five-step path of the Ignatian examen[24] resonates with the three moments in the trauma recovery process, and comparing the two journeys yields mutually enriching insight and practice. By way of overview, I redescribe the examen as the construction of a narrative that gathers, develops, evaluates, and directs threads of meaning in the events of daily life. The first two steps create a disposition of safety grounded in embracing an encompassing spirit of gratitude and articulating a desire to adopt a divine perspective on the day's events. The first step asks for gratitude for the gift of life and the opportunity to enter a closer union with the Triune God. The second step asks for the light of the Holy Spirit. This light brings a higher viewpoint to reorganize events under the divine illumination offered by self and even species transcending purpose. Both draw the examen's practitioners toward recognizing a safe context held and supported by a faithful and benevolent creator. The presupposition of the examen's worldview reinforces a sense of security within a friendly and ultimately safe universe.

The examen's third step involves a review of the day's events, plotting them into a narrative with direction, development, and purpose. The Greeks would describe this as a movement from *historia* to *theoria*, from a sequential enumeration of disconnected episodes to an account of an evaluative plot that identifies and assesses the flow of their interrelations and meaning.[25] *Theoria* means literally to reflect on the deep causality and significance of events. In the examen's context, *theoria* anticipates that the ebb and flow of events in the lives of individuals and communities express movements grounded in an originating source, run through developing dispositions, and yield outcomes to be evaluated with reference to a divine purpose. Of course, the activity implied by the creation of a story is no less important than the story itself. Crafting a narrative (re)activates the agency of the storyteller. It offers an opportunity to recognize, acknowledge, and reinforce the values implicated by the selection of events spun into the account. We return below to parse the significance of the activation of agency in the context of the movement from *historia* to *theoria*, the added value of participating in a religious narrative tradition and, particularly, the Christian narrative tradition.

Of course, the recalled events might sometimes resist being plotted into a constructive narrative. Some events are manifestly evil or at least apparently dissonant. Some events defy coming into the light, cast an imposing shadow, and even disrupt and distort the examen's assumed sense of basic safety. They threaten the disposition of gratitude and undermine the higher viewpoint we associate with the divine persons overlooking creation. The examen's fourth step acknowledges the darkness of personal, communal, institutional, and systemic evil and proposes the Paschal Mystery of Christ's death and resurrection in response.

The Paschal Mystery gathers and holds the suffering of individuals and communities under the light of a spiritual vision that eludes complete or even adequate definition and expression. The symbol of the cross retains an elemental meaning encountered and explored by people and communities over many historical epochs. The tradition reaches for notions of merit, redemption, vicarious suffering, and sacrifice to articulate how the light of the cross pushes back the darkness and completes the story about the flow of God's mercy and love.[26] Relocating moments of resistance and self-justification under the light of love radiating from the cross brings a new perspective that liberates agency and valorizes the denigrated persons and values assaulted by sin. The shame and confusion occasioned by one's own sin, the sin of another, or the structural sin of distorted social institutions yield to liberating sorrow.[27] The focus shifts from passive debilitation to the remediation of harm and the restoration of damaged social relations. The examen's story about the movement of the self advances toward completion, affirming reemerging agency, relocating the self as beloved but not the center of its own world, and setting the direction to act for a more just and merciful world. Discerning the direction of a spiritual movement and the impact of its fruit on individuals, communities, and the cascading webs of relationships in natural, social, cultural, and religious ecologies requires ongoing attention. The reemergence of personal agency, the restoration of social networks, and the reconstruction of cultural narratives are all positive indicators of closer participation and union in creation's higher purpose. While such restorations and confirmations of personal and collective agency are consoling signs, they also can be subject to distortions and ambiguities. As Ignatius wisely observes, not all things that follow consolation are of God.[28]

In discernment Ignatius advises us to pay attention to the nexus of source, development, and fruit. For Ignatius, knowledge of the source of a movement and its fruit are the most certain criteria for discernment.[29] For positive movements, this knowledge also remains tenuous. Close union with God eludes conceptualization, and the fruits of participation in higher divine purpose are future contingencies. Both require the reach of symbolization for reference and the stretch of metaphor for coherent sense.[30] The affordances and limitations of cultural and religious symbol systems shape all efforts to conceptualize and articulate the movement's source and fruit. Nonetheless, the reach of symbolization could inspire creative disruption and constructive social engagement. Coherent metaphors can shape an empowering spiritual vision of the final purpose that receives and validates the fruits.

Although Ignatius urges that the source, development, and fruit should equally be praiseworthy, intermediating objectives and the personal and social programs they inspire frequently become the de facto reference points for discernment. While the constructive contention between the source and the service of higher purpose holds these more concrete reference points, the development of dispositions is another significant touchpoint. In a dynamic, secularized, global context, the intermediating objectives are becoming harder to identify and less capable of attracting the broad recognition required to guide joint action. Dispositions may be an increasingly important forum for discernment and the intercultural and intergenerational spiritual conversations that support personal and communal discernment.

Within the context of personal discernment, the dispositions of the "First Principle and Foundation" that stand at the beginning of Ignatius's Spiritual Exercises—creaturely gratitude before the bounty of the Creator, freedom in the use of gifts and talents, and commitment in the service of divine purpose—are concrete resonances with the source and goal of positive spiritual movements.[31] These three—and especially the affective responses they elicit—serve as touchpoints for discernment. In communal discernment, the four Universal Apostolic Preferences arguably plays a similar role: Showing the way to God, walking with the poor in a mission of reconciliation and justice, accompanying young people in the creation of a hope-filled future, and collaborating in the care of our common home provide intermediary objectives that resonate with the contention of source and goal and inspire creative programmatic communal responses. Reconciliation is a spiritual gift and a social task. We do not save ourselves; God does not save us without us. When theology engages its living context, learned self-reflection guides the constructive contention of interior spiritual movements, shared religious meanings and values, and a well-informed social anthropology. Interior spiritual movements cultivate the shift from self-protection and self-promotion to freedom and willingness to serve a divine project eluding human control. Shared, ritualized religious meanings and values shape fallible human faith communities that advance and decline in their movements to a more just and merciful society. Social anthropology heightens self-critical awareness of the ambiguities of belonging that straighten and distort the journey's way. Cultivated in the learned context of Jesuit higher education, theology curates creative contentions and clears space for the conciliation of differences and the reconciliation of injustice.

Notes

1. Bernard Lonergan, "Sacralization and Secularization," in *Philosophical and Theological Papers, 1965–1980*, Collected Works of Bernard Lonergan, vol. 17, ed. Robert Croken (Toronto: University of Toronto Press, 2018), 259–81.

2. Arturo Sosa, SJ, "Discerning the Present to Prepare for the Future of the University Education of the Society of Jesus," in *The Catholic University as a Social Project,* ed. Michael J. Garanzini, SJ, and James P. McCartin (Washington, DC: Georgetown University Press, 2025), 9–24, https://www.jesuits.global/sj_files/2022/09/2022-08-04_IAJU-Speech_EN.pdf, accessed at August 1, 2025. For other discussions of secularism and modernity, see Craig Calhoun et al., eds., *Rethinking Secularism* (New York: Oxford University Press, 2011).

3. Charles Taylor, *A Secular Age* (Cambridge, MA: Belknap Press of Harvard University Press, 2007), 37–42.

4. For a discussion of this reframing of culture wars, see Randall S. Rosenberg, *The Givenness of Desire: Concrete Subjectivity and the Natural Desire to See God* (Toronto: University of Toronto Press, 2018), 190.

5. Clive Gamble, John Gowlett, and Robin Dunbar, *Thinking Big: How the Evolution of Social Life Shaped the Human Mind* (London: Thames & Hudson, 2014), 42.

6. R. Scott Appleby, *The Ambivalence of the Sacred: Religion, Violence, and Reconciliation* (Lanham, MD: Rowman & Littlefield, 2000).

7. Sosa, *Discerning the Present,* p. 9–24.

8. For a doctrinal affirmation of the right to culture see Second Vatican Council, "Pastoral Constitution on the Church in the Modern World," December 7, 1965, #60, https://www.vatican.va/archive/hist_councils/ii_vatican_council/documents/vat-ii_cons_19651207_gaudium-et-spes_en.html.

9. Gordon Rixon, "A Slain Lamb Standing: Journeying in Reconciliation," in *International Ignatian Reconciliation Conference: From Crisis and Confrontation to Healing and Forgiveness, How Is Reconciliation Possible?* (Bogotá: Editorial Pontificia Universidad Javeriana, 2022), 455–74.

10. Second Vatican Council, "Decree on the Apostolate of the Laity," February 18, 1965, #3, https://www.vatican.va/archive/hist_councils/ii_vatican_council/documents/vat-ii_decree_19651118_apostolicam-actuositatem_en.html.

11. See Congregation for the Doctrine of the Faith, *Dominus Iesus: Declaration on the Unicity and Salvific Universality of Jesus Christ and the Church* (Rome: Vatican Press Office, 2000), #4.

12. Hans Urs von Balthsar, *The Truth Is Symphonic: Aspects of Christian Pluralism* (San Francisco: Ignatius Press, 1987). For a discussion of the affordances and limitations of language, see Charles Taylor, *The Language Animal: The Full Shape of the Human Linguistic Capacity* (Cambridge, MA: Harvard University Press, 2016).

13. Pope Francis, "Evangelii Gaudium," November 24, 2013, ##115–118, https://www.vatican.va/content/francesco/en/apost_exhortations/documents/papa-francesco_esortazione-ap_20131124_evangelii-gaudium.html.

14. CBC News, "Remains of 215 Children Found Buried at Former B.C. Residential School, First Nation Says," May 28, 2021, https://www.cbc.ca/news/canada/british-columbia/tk-eml%C3%BAps-te-secw%C3%A9pemc-215-children-former-kamloops-indian-residential-school-1.6043778. See also J. S. Milloy, *A National Crime: The Canadian Government and the Residential School System, 1879–1986* (Winnipeg: University of Manitoba Press, 2017) and J. R. Miller, *Residential Schools and Reconciliation: Canada Confronts Its History* (Toronto: University of Toronto Press, 2017).

15. See the discussion of reconciliation and "meeting in council" in Pope Francis, "Meeting with Indigenous Peoples and Members of the Parish Community of Sacred Heart," Edmonton, July 25, 2022, https://www.vatican.va/content/francesco/en/speeches/2022/july/documents/20220725-incontroedmonton-canada.html

16. My discussion here follows Gordon Rixon, "The Church as Mission," University of Saint Michael's College, *InsightOut* Blog, November 27, 2023, https://stmikes.utoronto.ca/news/insightout-the-church-is-mission. For a discussion of the relation of the synodal process to the development of spiritual conversation, see Michael Higgins, "The Vatican Gathering Signals a New Approach for the Catholic Church," op. ed., *The Globe and Mail*, November 1, 2023, https://www.theglobeandmail.com/opinion/article-the-vatican-gathering-signals-a-new-approach-for-the-catholic-church/

17. XVI Ordinary General Assembly of the Synod of Bishops, *A Synodal Church in Mission: Synthesis Report*, October 28, 2023, 8, https://www.synod.va/en/news/a-synodal-church-in-mission.html

18. I am using the notion of contention as a constructive interaction of linked and opposed principles of activity in the sense of Robert Doran's "dialectic of contraries" and Romano Guardini's "polarité." See Robert M. Doran, *Theology and the Dialectics of History*

(Toronto: University of Toronto Press, 1990) and Romano Guardini, *La polarité: Essai d'une philosophie du vivant concret* (Paris: Éditions du Cerf, 2010).

19. For a fuller discussion of the missions in history, see Robert M. Doran, *The Trinity in History: A Theology of the Divine Missions* (Toronto University of Toronto Press, 2012).

20. For a discussion of the three dimensions of pilgrimage in the life of Ignatius of Loyola, see André Brouillette, "Le pèlerinage Ignatien: Entre ascèse, identité et mystique," *Nouvelle Revue Théologique* 140, no. 1 (2018): 91–106.

21. Sosa, *Discerning the Present,* p. 9–24.

22. My discussion of trauma follows Judith Herman, *Trauma and Recovery: The Aftermath of Violence—from Domestic Abuse to Political Terror* (New York: Basic Books, 2015). See also Bessel A. Van der Kolk, *The Body Keeps the Score: Brain, Mind, and Body in the Healing of Trauma* (New York: Penguin Books, 2015).

23. See Axel Honneth, *The Struggle for Recognition: The Moral Grammar of Social Conflicts* (Cambridge, MA: MIT Press, 1995).

24. *Spiritual Exercises,* #43.

25. For an example of the movement from *historia* to *theoria* in early Greek theology, see Gregory of Nyssa, *The Life of Moses* (Toronto: Paulist Press, 1978).

26. For a discussion of the complex efforts in the tradition to express the meaning of redemption, see Bernard Lonergan, "The Redemption," in *Philosophical and Theological Papers 1958–1964,* Collected Works of Bernard Lonergan, vol. 6, eds. Robert C. Croken, Frederick E. Crowe, and Robert M. Doran (Toronto: University of Toronto Press, 1996), 14–24.

27. *Spiritual Exercises,* #48, #55.

28. *Spiritual Exercises,* #332.

29. Ignatius proposes three times for making a decision, including a time of such intimate union that sure decisions can be made, *Spiritual Exercises,* #175. For a discussion, see Robert M. Doran, "Ignatian Themes in the Thought of Bernard Lonergan: Revisiting a Topic That Deserves Further Reflection," *Lonergan Workshop* 19 (2006): 82–106.

30. For a discussion of the role of symbol and metaphor in the development of the sense and reference of language, see Paul Ricoeur, *Interpretation Theory: Discourse and the Surplus of Meaning* (Fort Worth: Texas Christian University Press, 1976).

31. *Spiritual Exercises,* #23.

5

Discerning a Hope-Filled Future

Some Insights from Liberation Psychology

Jennifer Abe

Introduction: The Challenge
of Kindling Hope

IN SPRING 2023 I TAUGHT an in-person seminar on liberation psychology for graduating seniors. It was my first semester back after finishing a term as a senior administrator at my institution; my responsibilities had included guiding our university's responses in the wake of the murder of George Floyd and other innocent Black people up to and including 2020. The ensuing societal reckoning with racial injustice gained momentum during the COVID-19 pandemic, a time that itself brought the fragility of our collective existence into acute awareness. By the time I returned to my department, I had seen how my colleagues across the university had mobilized in heroic ways, big and small, as they coped with the consequences of the pandemic and the challenges of systemic racism. I also observed how little opportunity they had to heal and to reconnect with one another once we all returned to campus. Even though we were finally able to share physical spaces together, albeit often in modified ways, our work as staff and faculty seemed more demanding and difficult than ever. The sense of depletion, burnout, and demoralization was palpable, and the need to restore a sense of community, profound.

For many of us at Jesuit institutions, recovering a sense of shared purpose, community, and belonging in a radically altered social reality remains a critical challenge. A continuing widespread sense of disconnection and the alarming consequences of societal disparities, global warming, and political polarization have made it clear that we need to reimagine what we are to become as we move into the future. In facing these social and environmental challenges in ways that are true to our core values and institutional missions, how do we continue to draw deeply from our Ignatian tradition, one that has so animated and sustained others over the past five hundred years?

It is with these concerns in mind that I approach Father Sosa's 2022 address on Jesuit higher education in which he exhorts us to "grow as institutions that form persons who are integral and integrated, able to discern the present as long as they live and committed to the search for social and ecological justice."[1] Father Sosa's holistic view of social and ecological justice is nested within Pope Francis's vision of "integral ecology" in *Laudato Si'*, where he observes that "we are not faced with two separate crises, one environmental and the other social, but rather one complex crisis which is both social and environmental."[2] In response, Father Sosa proposes an integrated vision for our Jesuit institutions that asks us to educate students to "help pave the way to a more just society with fraternal relations among persons, their cultures, peoples, and nations . . . the common good . . . reconciliation with the environment, reestablishing an equilibrium . . . that promotes not only the full life of all human persons but also life itself on planet Earth."[3]

Father Sosa also challenges Jesuit institutions to reconsider our own "way of proceeding."[4] Specifically, he invites our institutions to become spaces that enable discernment, inhabiting our distinctive place in society by learning to "read the signs of the times," able to help move our world toward a hope-filled future.[5] In calling us to recommit to the tradition of Ignatian discernment, Father Sosa asks us to clarify the focus of our institutional work and identity, especially with regard to the contributions we hope to make within our specific cultural and national contexts. He invites us to engage with our societies to allow for nothing less than the transformation of how we orient to one other and to the natural world. These questions invite us to consider how we, as Jesuit institutions of higher education, might effectively "accompany young people in the creation of a hope-filled future" in the spirit of the Universal Apostolic Preferences of the Society of Jesus.[6]

So, how might our institutions more deeply engage practices of Ignatian discernment to enact the values of solidarity, dialogue, and collaboration that Father Sosa lifts up in his address? Clearly there is a need to do so, in a context where we so often find ourselves discouraged and even hopeless from our ongoing struggles with social and environmental issues. From this place and in this time, we are challenged to find ways forward that can rekindle hope, especially for the sake of our students.

Many persons, especially young people, are impatient to see if we can build the kind of collective agency required to reorient ourselves to each other and the world in a different way. Such a shared commitment to action would contribute hope to their lives not only for the future but also now in the present. Some might question whether hope is even important at a time when the need for action is so urgent. What does it even mean to live with hope? Theologian Miroslav Volf writes, "In hope, a future good which isn't yet, somehow already is. A future good we cannot see, which waits in darkness, still qualifies our entire existence."[7] It may well be that hope "waits in the darkness" of our time and that we must patiently seek out and trust what is already somehow present. But the spiritual and existential questions accompanying this challenging period are pressing. From another perspective, psychologist C. R. Snyder and his colleagues propose that in addition to having goals, individual hope contains two critical elements: a perceived pathway forward (planning to meet goals) and a sense of agency (goal-directed determination).[8] As a society, it seems that we often can indeed envision the paths we must take to address our goals, the pressing concerns of our time, and we even understand the existential urgency to do so. But will we do so? Can we do so? The discouragement and demoralization may come not so much from the perceived lack of pathways forward but from real questions about whether we have the collective human agency to do so.

One thing seems clear: If we are to locate the collective hope needed to fuel such action, we must find this hope together. In the service of this project, I want to propose some insights from liberation psychology, a field that makes visible the critical connection between personal well-being and social transformation toward justice, a commitment consistent with our efforts at Jesuit institutions to prepare "integral and integrated persons" capable of living in "well-educated solidarity."[9] Making these connections between personal and collective experience must be supported within institutional structures, which is why I also want to consider what it might mean for Jesuit institutions to become spaces of discernment in the service of a hope-filled future. Finally, I want to examine what it will mean for us at Jesuit institutions to connect hope to action through our pedagogy and practices.

Liberation Psychology, Mental Health, and Spirituality in the Present Moment

The field of liberation psychology was founded by Father Ignacio Martín-Baró, SJ, one of the six Jesuits who, along with their housekeeper and her daughter, were murdered in 1989 at their home, the Jesuit university in San Salvador during El Salvador's civil war. Martín-Baró was also a social psychologist who, given his training, position, and experience in Latin America, took seriously the precepts of liberation theology to create a vision of psychology that turned toward a new horizon, one that centered the realities of those living on the margins of society. His work was closely aligned with that of Paolo Freire, who influenced

Martin-Baró's insistence on the importance of nurturing "critical consciousness" among the oppressed.[10] The notion of critical consciousness contextualized the lived experience of the oppressed within their broader social, political, and historical realities. By doing so, Freire argued, the oppressed could learn to "read the word" of their existence, interpreting their lived experience with greater agency, empowering them for action. For Freire, critical consciousness also meant "learning to say the word of one's own existence, which is personal but, more significantly, collective," so that those who were oppressed could feel the value of their individual and communal ways of knowing, asking critical questions of the society of which they were a part.[11]

For the oppressed to "read" and "say" the word of their existence entails learning to assert their own value and agency in systems that too often dehumanize and devalue them. The *intersectionality* of an individual's identity also means that these lived experiences of dehumanization and oppression are expressed in ways particular to the configuration of one's different identities and to what they signify within a given social and cultural context.[12] Further, because our lives are embedded within systems that reinforce inequities between different groups in society, the interdependence of economic, political, and social structures also contributes to these experiences of dehumanization and oppression. Awareness of the interconnected nature of this experience, between what is personal (identity) and what is collective (group inequities), is critical to liberation psychology. Fannie Lou Hamer famously asserted, "Nobody's free until everybody's free" in a speech she gave in 1971, providing a central insight into the nature of our interconnectedness.[13]

To see this interconnected vision of reality is to recognize that our shared existence as living beings on earth requires living into our interdependent realities, including with nonhuman living beings, as a collective commitment. As Father Sosa notes, what is at stake is "[not only] the full life of all human persons, but also life itself on planet Earth." The invitation here means committing ourselves to living with love and justice in order to truly "speak the word"—in all the nuances, beauty, and pain of our distinctive, particular realities—of our shared existence in this world.

Yet can we and will we do so? Responding to this spiritual invitation also acknowledges that the social and existential threats to our collective future add to the complexity and challenge of addressing a profound crisis in mental health, especially among our young people. The Centers for Disease Control issued its 2022 summary of Youth Risk Behaviors Survey data, which indicated disturbing increases in negative mental health outcomes and thoughts of suicide among young people between 2011 and 2021, with more than 40 percent of high school students reporting "feeling so sad or hopeless that they could not engage in their regular activities . . . in the past year."[14] Globally, in a study of over eighty thousand youth, rates of depression and anxiety more than doubled during the pandemic.[15] Emergency room visits for suicide attempts have also increased substantially, especially among adolescent girls.[16] These statistics are alarming and provide compelling testimony to rising levels of psychological distress among our young people.

At the same time, we also need to pay attention to the ways in which broader social factors are associated with this individual distress. Former U.S. Surgeon General Vivek Murthy also drew attention, for instance, to the negative impacts of social media on the mental health of young people.[17] He urged more systematic efforts to rebuild a sense of community and strengthen social connection in order to combat the widespread loneliness, disconnection, and sense of isolation that are affecting the country. There is a call here to "hold the whole," to knit together the individual and collective, and to recognize the need for both personal and social healing for a crisis that is both psychological and spiritual in nature.[18] One of the students in my liberation psychology capstone seminar wrote a reflection that illuminates this holistic frame:

Recently, I have had moments where I become overwhelmed when I witness all of the tragic and violent events that are happening all over the world. This overwhelming feeling diminishes my hope because it feels like all of the bad things in the world will consume me and that there can be no resolutions to these issues. For example, I often worry about events of climate change, gun violence, and war that I read about on the news. These large, terrible events make me feel hopeless because it makes me think about how pointless our daily positive experiences are when the world is not at peace on a larger scale.

It is sobering to read these words and to feel the sense of anxiety and fear they contain. But it also gives new urgency to the question: Can we really afford to view the mental health concerns of our students in a way that does not take seriously both personal and collective realities? When I ask my students, they tell me that a more holistic perspective makes them feel seen in their experience of the world, and less stigmatized in feeling anxiety, depression, and even despair, in response. This frame helps opens a space where they can imagine themselves more fully and deeply, relating their experiences to a broader collective reality.

Expanding our imaginative reach—which is a big part of what liberation psychology has done for me and my students—can facilitate envisioning what healing might look like at different levels, not only at the personal level but also at the social, political, and even ecological levels. What might this imaginative work do to aid us in creating multilevel institutional responses, so that we think about healing as more than increasing mental health services to address student need, as important as this is? We could pay greater attention to a wider range of intentionally complementary institutional practices, in addition to mental health services. For example:

(1) offering spaces and opportunities for students to strengthen social connectedness, a sense of belonging, and to increase critical consciousness. Engaging in deep listening, dialogue, community-building, and

> other restorative practices could be part of what happens in these spaces;
>
> (2) engaging in sustainable, just, and fair practices as part of our institutional commitment and organizational cultures to both hold ourselves accountable and model global citizenship; and
>
> (3) connecting our universities with neighboring communities and the natural world in ways that nurture a sense of place and promote practices of mutuality, reciprocity, care, and respect.

Engaging in the work of personal and collective healing in such ways allows us to live into our values for meeting our students where they are, aligning with the Ignatian values that are at the heart of our university missions. Ideals and values such as the *cura personalis* (care of the whole person) and *cura apostolica* (care for our institutions and our shared work within them), along with Father Sosa's call to help form "integral and integrated" persons capable of living in "well-educated solidarity," can resonate with renewed force and meaning if we attend to them in a variety of contexts and through a variety of practices.

Paying attention to the whole, to our desire to "educate the whole person," also meets a deep hunger in young people today. According to the 2021 Springtide Report, for example, "young people are attempting to experience a wholeness and connection that demands curiosity and flexibility if they are to stay true to [who] they understand themselves to be."[19] What young people most yearn for, it seems, is a sense of wholeness, in which they can experience their integrity and authenticity, and spirituality is clearly an important part of this wholeness. Growing evidence suggests that young people are "unbundling" different forms of spiritual practice to "integrate their existing multiplicities" outside of formal faith traditions and religious institutional structures, identifying as "spiritual, but not religious." In fact, one of the fastest-growing categories of spiritual identity among young people is known as the "nones"—a group of people whose spirituality is not tied to any kind of religious affiliation.[20]

To recognize and respect that spirituality, in its broadest and most inclusive sense, can be expressed both within religious traditions and outside these formal boundaries, is a critical part of our work with students. Though it is important that we at Jesuit institutions make available the substantial resources of Ignatian spirituality on our campuses, the invitation to a deeper spiritual practice is not conditional: It does not require identifying as Catholic or even as persons of faith. Instead, this invitation entails on the one hand, a digging inward and downward into the bedrock of our core values to find a ground that can sustain us individually and collectively, and on the other hand, using our individual and collective imaginations to gaze outward and upward, locating our guiding aspirations and inspirations.

Discerning the Present to Prepare for the Future: Hope and Healing

The desire for a sense of wholeness runs deep among our students, and is echoed in Father Sosa's call to make the university a space for discernment to "accompany the processes of a great variety of persons who are living different moments of their lives."[21] Again, here is one of my students:

> It is one thing to hear tragic stories on the news, but it is another to know the struggles of people I personally know. Today, I have very few friends who have not been diagnosed with either anxiety or depression. I know people who have or are currently struggling with drug addiction, and I have spoken to their loved ones who do not understand how to help and are struggling to cope with the situation. Sometimes, thinking about these issues would diminish my hope, especially when my mind could not come up with any solutions. It is incredibly hard to see loved ones suffer and feel like all you can do is watch. And of course, my own personal struggles set

> me back as well. There are days that I fear for my future, I
> stress when I lose my sense of direction, I become depressed
> when obstacles in my life seem to stretch for an eternity, while
> the high I feel from my successes are gone in a millisecond.

"Fear for my future" reflects just one of the troubling consequences of these struggles: the sense that that time is foreshort-
ened, that we cannot see the way ahead. But it reveals something
important about our relationship with time in constructing our
very identity.[22] Psychological research suggests when a person's
sense of having a future is cut short, whether through stress, uncertainty, or other negative conditions beyond one's control,
negative mental health outcomes often follow, and a sense of
hope is greatly diminished.[23] Despair and apathy are at the op-
posite pole from hope, as are helplessness and hopelessness.[24]
The question that emerges for me, with ever greater urgency, is:
How can we learn to cultivate hope, in a way that can help us
move toward healing and wholeness?

One helpful response to this question comes from the research of Della Mosley and her colleagues (2020), who, in response to the needs of communities of color in fighting societal
injustice and historical oppression, have developed a psychological model for *radical hope*.[25] Their framework of radical hope
includes the goal of *radical healing* that involves "becoming
whole in the face of historical and ongoing experiences of oppression."[26] Radical hope, understood in this way, anchors
hope in time, to both past and future, and also connects individual and collective aspects of experience. At the individual level,
the sense of being connected across time to one's ancestors and
forebears can feed hope and increase motivation for individuals
as they learn to embrace ancestral pride (past) and find meaning
and purpose (future). At the collective level, communities can
draw strength from understanding their history of oppression
and resistance (past) and in envisioning possibilities for what
they want to create in moving forward (future). In this model,
holding a long view of time and staying connected to one's

community are both critical to sustaining radical hope, especially when change can feel so slow. Here, we find ourselves invited to consider how we can draw sustenance from the work of those who came before, to connect to others in solidarity in the present, and to continue to dream and enact what is possible for a shared future. And although this model of radical hope was designed with societal oppression in mind, I believe that it can also speak to the long-term perspective that is required to combat climate change, as well.

This intentional anchoring in time is already part of the diverse cultural and spiritual traditions that shape many of our lives. The African sankofa symbol, for example, with the head of a large bird facing backward across its body and its feet facing forward, is a source of inspiration in many African American communities. The way the sankofa reaches back into the past to retrieve what is needed by the community—both in the present and in the desired future—offers an important image of hope.[27] Many religious traditions, including Judaism, Christianity, and Islam, also speak to a sense of a fluid relationship between past, present, and future, with rituals that allow the past to become powerfully alive in the present moment: for example, Passover, which commemorates the exodus from Egypt; the Easter Vigil, which welcomes Christ's resurrection; and Eid ul-Fitr, which marks the end of Ramadan. These celebrations gather stories from the past to hold and lift up a religious community in the present moment. And whether these rituals and ceremonies honor the wisdom of our ancestors, the foundational stories of our faith traditions, or the pioneering work of contemporary social and environmental activists, they draw on collective memory to strengthen a community's identity in a way that helps sustain them for their future. These practices also illumine how past, present, and future are not reducible to chronological time but are activated in our imaginations, colliding and connecting us in different ways.

While it can be consoling to be reminded that the past holds rich resources that can strengthen us for the work ahead, it is also critical to recognize that collective memory can elicit guilt and shame in relation to the past. Psychological research suggests that we are motivated to forget our collective past or even make an explicit break with this history when it feels threatening to our social identity.[28] In such instances, our collective memory and dominant cultural narratives may be marked by gaps, silences, revisions, and smoothing over—a collective denial, as if nothing ever happened. Here, the anguish of the psalmist and language of reckoning, lamentations, and repentance in the Christian tradition, as well as in other religious traditions, can give us a rich vocabulary for facing the past and incorporating its painful elements into our present identity.[29]

What is noteworthy here is that the nonlinear aspects of time expose how we may not so much "move past" the past as much as we need to fully digest and integrate it into our present. Recovering this kind of historical memory is part of the work that psychologist Kari Grain (2022), a scholar of *critical hope*, refers to as the excavation of "difficult knowledge."[30] Opening oneself up, whether personally or as a member of a larger community, to such difficult knowledge is complex, ambiguous, and often painful. Such openness has the potential, however, to "transform the very boundaries of who we are, because we cannot continue to be the same."[31]

At times we might ask ourselves: Do we really want our boundaries to be so transformed? Father Sosa observes, "to discern requires accepting challenges . . . challenges that often frighten us, with good reason."[32] A space of discernment implies risk, representing an encounter with the "Other" that might gift us with "difficult knowledge" that we might not welcome. Yet this kind of encounter, Sosa contends, also holds the power to transform us toward greater wholeness, helping us "to overcome the tendencies to fragmentation" within society.[33] How might we encourage a practice of openness so that we are able to share and to receive that which is offered to us? How do we create hospitable spaces that invite such transformation?

Anchoring Hope in Practice: Participating in the Ongoing Creation of the World

An openness to transformation is a necessary foundation for our way of proceeding within Jesuit institutions. Only then will we also be able to invite our students into an educational experience that will help them, and all of us, move toward "the full life of all human persons . . . [and] life itself on planet Earth."[34] Moving toward life in all its possibility reflects an act of faith, as well as an expression of hope. In his writings, Paolo Freire asserted that hope needs action to be sustained, that "[w]ithout a minimum of hope, we cannot so much as start the struggle. But without the struggles, hope, as an ontological need, dissipates, loses its bearings, and turns into hopelessness."[35] As such, we need to be intentional about cultivating hope through action. In considering how to activate this vital connection between action and hope, we can see ourselves anew, as participating in the work of "ongoing creation."[36]

Participation in the work of ongoing creation has been described by Douglas Christie (2013), a theologian writing about contemplative ecology, as "practicing paradise," in which we "imagine the world as whole, inhabit it with tenderness and care, and contribute to its renewal."[37] This represents just one way that contemporary theologians are beginning to think about this important work. Imagining the world as whole and contributing to its renewal are also central to Jewish religious thought, beautifully captured in the paired concepts of *tikkun nefesh*, repair of our souls, and *tikkun olam,* repair of the world.[38] Here, I think we in Jesuit higher education might benefit from reimagining the Ignatian tradition of discernment as a dual practice that invites us to face both inward, attending to the inner movements of the soul, and outward, toward the work of God in the world. Indeed, an outward-oriented discernment may be viewed as a form of critical consciousness that helps us to "read the signs of the times" through the eyes of faith. It also enables us to connect to radical hope, learning to see the work of God in time, anchored in the past and connected to the future. Philosopher James K. A. Smith views this dynamic process of broader discernment as a practice of "temporal faithfulness," or becoming attentive to the imprint of God's grace and the Spirit's action in the world through time.[39] Including in our own time.

This work of temporal faithfulness, whether understood as practicing paradise, restoring the world, or as an outward-facing discernment, involves not merely *seeing* God's work in time but *participating* in it. That is, to engage in the work of social and ecological justice, in the work healing ourselves and the world, is to participate in the work of the Spirit in the world in our historical time, moving always toward life in all its fullness. Such deeply engaged participation requires the work of the imagination—learning to *imagine* the world as whole and participating in the creation of a world that is healed and restored. In this work, we come to see ourselves simultaneously as fully responsible for our actions in our time and fragile, finite strands in a broader weaving of divine action and grace across time. This imaginative perspective can help to foreground the work of ongoing creation in the world and the invitation we are given to participate in it. Participation thus becomes crucial in learning how to live *with* hope and *into* hope. And because participation always means showing up, it becomes an expression of faithfulness to being present and available for what is needed.

To participate, then, is to link hope with action, action that also connects us with others in this shared work. One of the students in my capstone course expressed what it means for her to find hope in this way:

> While my awareness of current worldly problems is increasing, so is my awareness of possibilities for healing in the future. I am hearing more stories of people who have successfully overcome their childhood trauma, who are continually growing and learning how to take their power back. People who are fighting ongoing battles with mental illness but becoming increasingly efficient at managing and coping with their symptoms.

> I have seen and experienced the immense benefits of having a strong support system, and seeing how many people benefit from that gives me hope. . . . The more I see others building a hope-filled future for themselves, the more vivid my own becomes.

As this student's reflection suggests, the relationship between hope and action, between us and others, is both reciprocal and synergistic: To participate is to receive hope from the actions of others as well as to create hope for others through our own actions.

Father Sosa speaks of discernment as a "pedagogy of grace."[40] But should we not also orient toward hope with a "pedagogy of possibility"? It seems to me that while we are often highly attuned to helping our students gain an awareness and deep understanding of the challenges of social, political, and ecological issues in the world, we do not always put in as much effort to point to the actions that can give hope, what change (whether big or small) actually looks like in this moment, as it is unfolding in the world. How can we help our students see not only that action is possible but that actions are already happening all around us? We want them to bear witness to how people are in this very moment, and in many different ways, creatively and imaginatively participating in the work of restoring the world, of practicing paradise. These are the stories, practices, and models that can help us build hope. Is it really ethical in our time to teach in a way that does not include such envisioning for the future? Do we not owe our students these varied pathways to help them imagine a future for themselves?

In closing I offer the idea that framing our lives as an expression of how we participate in the ongoing creation of the world can help us in our shared work. This sense of participation in the world, as part of the world, is very different than assuming an outrageously heavy burden and sense of responsibility to "save the world," especially as a consequence of the folly and irresponsibility of previous generations. Instead, participation allows us to fully inhabit our commitment and desire to work together toward ecological and social justice, even if we feel outraged at how we, as humans, came to this place of reckoning with our multiple crises, and despite the fact that we, as individuals, will not fully reap the benefits ourselves. In this sense, participation also invokes humility, a recognition of our finitude in that we do not, and cannot, know the end of the story of the world, just as others before us could not see how their parts of this story were woven into the larger whole.

And the story is not yet finished, no matter how we may feel. Our commitment to participate in the ongoing creation of the world can become an important element of our basis for hope—for collectively asserting our existential fight against learned helplessness, a shared refusal of hopelessness, and a communal defense against despair. Our commitment to hope and participation in the life of the world can form the foundation for collective action. Not because we are so confident that all our efforts will be successful—after all, hope is not the same as optimism—but because our actions themselves reflect our ontological need as human beings to express ourselves as fully alive in the world. We choose to participate in the world, working toward its healing and wholeness, because we desire to move toward life, and the fullness of living, as part of this living world.

This is the invitation for those of us working in Jesuit institutions—to educate students into this well-educated solidarity, to help them find who they are and what they bring, as integral and integrated persons, to their participation in the ongoing creation and restoration of the world. Responding to Father Sosa's call will indeed help them, and us, to "always move towards life in all its fullness." And to live into a hope-filled future.

Notes

1. Arturo Sosa, SJ, "Discerning the Present to Prepare for the Future of the University Education of the Society of Jesus," in *The Catholic University as a Social Project,* ed. Michael J. Garanzini, SJ, and James P.

McCartin (Washington, DC: Georgetown University Press, 2025), 9–24.

2. Catholic Church. Pope Francis, *Laudato Si': On Care for Our Common Home: Encyclical Letter* (Vatican City, Rome, 2015), https://www.vatican.va/content/francesco/en/encyclicals/documents/papa-francesco_20150524_enciclica-laudato-si.html

3. Sosa, *Discerning the Present,* p. 9–24.

4. Sosa, *Discerning the Present,* p. 9–24.

5. Sosa, *Discerning the Present,* p. 9–24.

6. Arturo Sosa, SJ, *Universal Apostolic Preferences of the Society of Jesus, 2019–2029* (Rome: Society of Jesus, 2019), 1–10, https://www.jesuits.global/sj_files/2020/05/2019-06_19feb19_eng.pdf

7. Miroslav Volf, *Theologies of Hope* (New Haven, CT: Yale Center for Faith and Culture, 2020), https://reflections.yale.edu/article/seeking-light-notes-hope/theologies-hope

8. Charles R. Snyder, C. Harris, J. R. Anderson, et al., "The Will and the Ways: Development and Validation of an Individual-Differences Measure of Hope," *Journal of Personality and Social Psychology* 60, no. 4 (1991): 570–585. https://doi.org/10.1037/0022-3514.60.4.570

9. Sosa, *Discerning the Present,* p. 9–24.

10. Paolo Freire, *Pedagogy of the Oppressed* (New York: Continuum, 1990).

11. Quoted in Father Ignacio Martin-Baró, SJ, *Writings for a Liberation Psychology* (Cambridge, MA: Harvard University Press, 1996), 40.

12. Kimberle Crenshaw, "Demarginalizing the Intersection of Race and Sex: A Black Feminist Critique of Antidiscrimination Doctrine, Feminist Theory and Antiracist Politics," in *Feminist Legal Theory: Foundations,* ed. D. K. Weisberg (Philadelphia: Temple University Press, 1993), 383–95.

13. Fannie Lou Hamer, "'Nobody's Free Until Everybody's Free': Speech Delivered at the Founding of the National Women's Political Caucus, Washington, DC, July 10, 1971," in *The Speeches of Fannie Lou Hamer: To Tell It Like It Is,* ed. Maegan Parker Brooks and Davis W. Houck (Oxford: University Press of Mississippi, 2010), 134–39.

14. Centers for Disease Control and Prevention, *The Youth Risk Behavior Survey Data Summary & Trends Report: 2011–2021,* (2022), https://www.cdc.gov/yrbs/index.html

15. Nicole Racine, Brae Ann McArthur, Jessica E. Cooke, Rachel Eirich, Jenney Zhu, and Sheri Madigan, "Global Prevalence of Depressive and Anxiety Symptoms in Children and Adolescents During COVID-19: A Meta-Analysis," *JAMA Pediatrics* 175, no. 11 (2021): 1142–50. https://doi.org/10.1001/jamapediatrics.2021.2482

16. Centers for Disease Control and Prevention, *Youth Risk Behavior Surveillance Data Summary & Trends Report: 2009–2019*, (2020).

17. Vivek H. Murthy, "Surgeon General: We Have Become a Lonely Nation. It's Time to Fix That," *New York Times*, April 30, 2023, https://www.nytimes.com/2023/04/30/opinion/loneliness-epidemic -america.html

18. Editorial, "There's a Mental Crisis Among Teens. The Catholic Church Needs to Respond," *America Magazine*, April 20, 2023, https://www.americamagazine.org/politics-society/2023/04/20/teen -mental-health-crisis-faith-245122

19. Springtide Research Institute, *The State of Religion & Young People: Navigating Uncertainty* (Winona, MN, 2021).

20. Pew Research Center, "A Close Look at America's Rapidly Growing Religious 'Nones' (2015), https://www.pewresearch.org/short-reads /2015/05/13/a-closer-look-at-americas-rapidly-growing-religious -nones/

21. Sosa, *Discerning the Present*, p. 9–24.

22. Phillip Zimbardo and John Boyd, *The Time Paradox: The New Psychology of Time That Will Change Your Life* (New York: Free Press, 2008).

23. Torgrim Gjesme, "On the Concept of Future Time Orientation: Considerations of Some Functions and Measurements' Implications," *International Journal of Psychology* 18, nos. 1–4 (1983), 443–461, https://doi.org/10.1080/00207598308247493

24. Casey Gwinn and Chan Hellman, *Hope Rising: How the Science of Hope Can Change Your Life* (New York: Morgan James, 2022), 61–68.

25. Della V. Mosley, Helen A. Neville, Nayeli Y. Chavez-Dueñas, Hector Y. Adames, Jioni A. Lewis, and Bryana H. French, "Radical Hope in Revolting Times: Proposing a Culturally Relevant Psychological Framework," *Social and Personality Psychology Compass* 14, no. 1 (2020). https://doi.org/10.1111/spc3.12512

26. Mosley et al., 3.

27. Cheryl Grills and Martin Ajei, "African-Centered Conceptualizations of Self and Consciousness: The Akan Model," in *Counseling Persons of African Descent: Raising the Bar of Practitioner Competence*, ed. T. A. Parham (Thousand Oaks: Sage, 2002), 75–99. https://doi.org /10.4135/9781452229119.n6

28. Katie Rotella and Jennifer Richardson, "Motivated to 'Forget': The Effects of In-Group Wrongdoing on Memory and Collective Guilt," *Social Psychological and Personality Science* 4, no. 6 (2013), 730–737. https://doi.org/10.1177/1948550613482986; Gilad Hirschberger,

"Collective Trauma and the Social Construction of Meaning," *Frontiers in Psychology* 9 (2018): 1441, https://doi.org/10.3389/fpsyg.2018.01441

29. Bessel van der Kolk, *The Body Keeps the Score: Brain, Mind, and Body in the Healing of Trauma* (London: Penguin, 2015); Helene Shulman and Mary Watkins, *Toward Psychologies of Liberation* (London: Palgrave Macmillan, 2008).

30. Kari Grain, *Critical Hope: How to Grapple with Complexity, Lead with Purpose, and Cultivate Transformative Social Change* (Berkeley, CA: North Atlantic Books, 2022).

31. Grain, 72.

32. Sosa, *Discerning the Present*, p. 9–24.

33. Sosa, *Discerning the Present*, p. 9–24.

34. Sosa, *Discerning the Present*, p. 9–24.

35. Paolo Freire, *Pedagogy of Hope: Reliving Pedagogy of the Oppressed* (New York: Continuum, 1994), 3.

36. Elizabeth A. Johnson, *Quest for the Living God: Mapping Frontiers in the Theology of God* (London: Bloomsbury Academic, 2007).

37. Douglas Christie, *The Blue Sapphire of the Mind: Notes for a Contemplative Ecology* (Oxford, UK: Oxford University Press, 2013), 314.

38. Shulman and Watkins, 335.

39. James K. A. Smith, *How to Inhabit Time: Understanding the Past, Facing the Future, Living Faithfully Now* (Ada, MI: Brazos Press, 2022).

40. Sosa, *Discerning the Present*, p. 9–24.

6

Transcending Generations and Cultures

The True Meaning of the Lord of Heaven and Jesuit Higher Education Today

ELEONORE STUMP

Introduction

FR. SOSA'S ADDRESS IS RICH and stimulating, and it reminds us forcefully of the power and the beauty of the Jesuit mission. In this brief reflection, I cannot begin to do justice to the myriad strands of Fr. Sosa's address and the many serious challenges it presents. Here I want to focus on just one of those strands, namely, the tensions Fr. Sosa calls to our attention between, as he says, the history that has made Jesuit colleges and universities what they are and want to be and our complicated current times with all their complex demands. I will concentrate on the themes of intergenerationality and interculturality, which Fr. Sosa emphasizes as the best hope for resolving the tensions that concern him.

Intergenerationality

One way to think of intergenerationality is as a matter of the transmission of the tradition of a worldview or culture. Our word "tradition" comes, of course, from the Latin word *traditio*, which means *handing on*, especially the handing on from one generation to another of the culture and knowledge built up within a civilization. The process of handing on enables one generation to benefit from the insights and endeavors of previous generations, and it keeps each new generation from having to start *ab initio* to acquire those things that make human life more than merely animal.

Our own age has been particularly concerned to ensure the handing on of scientific knowledge. It is clear to us that science is a communal enterprise, and we have developed efficient, technologically sophisticated means for transmitting the methods, procedures, and results of one generation of scientists to the next. In learning from the work of previous generations of scientific researchers, we may find that we have to revise or even reject some of what they had accepted; but we make progress in science because we have first learned from the communal expertise of those generations of scientific researchers who have gone before.

It is clear that the same point applies to human civilization more broadly conceived. No culture completely divorced from its common past can flourish, as the sad lessons of the twentieth century show, because human expertise is vested in an intergenerational community that is extended across times. In the West, the two millennia of the Christian era have yielded a wealth of work in philosophy and theology and the other humanistic disciplines. The intellectual heritage of this era encapsulates the communal experience of many generations of thinkers who in varying degrees succeeded or failed in the enterprise of understanding and living a Christian worldview.

Both in its brilliant successes and in its failures, this intellectual heritage has a great deal to teach us. It is clear that even a moderate acquaintance with it can yield a deeper understanding of the Christian worldview and a more powerful commitment to living it in service of others in our world. And as the Christian tradition itself has supposed, it is the task of every generation to develop as well as to hand on the heritage it has received.[1] Many of the most pressing problems of our age can be addressed more insightfully by making use of the communal expertise embodied in this tradition, as Fr. Sosa's address itself exemplifies.

One might suppose, then, that it would be relatively easy to argue for the centrality of this intellectual heritage in Jesuit universities, whose mission statements generally emphasize the centrality of the Jesuit Christian worldview. For example, the mission statement of my own university, Saint Louis University, begins this way:

> The Mission of Saint Louis University is the pursuit of truth for the greater glory of God and for the service of humanity. The University seeks excellence in the fulfillment of its corporate purposes of teaching, research, health care and service to the community. It is dedicated to leadership in the continuing quest for understanding of God's creation and for the discovery, dissemination and integration of the values, knowledge and skills required to transform society in the spirit of the Gospels. As a Catholic, Jesuit university, this pursuit is motivated by the inspiration and values of the Judeo-Christian tradition and is guided by the spiritual and intellectual ideals of the Society of Jesus.

But, in fact, the idea that one can integrate the Christian intellectual heritage with standard secular academic study is now met with suspicion, if not outright opposition, by some faculty and administrators even in Jesuit universities. In addition to the increasing secularization of many universities, in recent decades there has also been an emphasis on the need to acquaint students with the worldviews of cultures in non-Christian and non-Western parts of the world. These developments can serve as a corrective to the provincialism that was sometimes characteristic of some areas of the humanities in Western universities in the past. But they also can have the effect of divorcing even many educated Christians who study and work in Jesuit universities from the Christian tradition. Between the growth of the sciences and the turn to multiculturalism in the humanities, the tradition, the intergenerationality, of the great Christian intellectual heritage has suffered.

Intergenerationality: The External Challenge

One challenge to the integration of the Christian intellectual tradition into the educational structures of Jesuit universities thus comes from those who question whether it is even possible for scholarship and Christian conviction to mix. On the face of it, this might seem to be an odd question. Widespread atheism among intellectuals is a fairly recent phenomenon in the West. Scholarship of all sorts has been characteristic of Christianity almost from its inception; and for most of Christian history, intellectually inclined thinkers would have supposed that there is an obvious affirmative answer to the question whether Christianity and scholarship can mix. Since the Enlightenment, however, many people have supposed the right answer is "No, they can't!"

Enlightenment thinkers believed that all reputable learning is a universal or generically human enterprise. This belief is part of a view sometimes called modernism. In academia, modernists have thought, we should put aside all our particularities—of gender, race, nationality, religion, and social class—and enter into the project of learning just as the generic human beings we are. And that is why modernists thought Christianity and reputable academic work do not mix. On modernist views, mixing Christianity with scholarship just wrecks the scholarship.

In reaction to this Enlightenment view, recent years have seen the rise of what has been called "postmodernism." For postmodernists, it is only pretense to present any scholarship as generically human in character; all of it is done from the vantage point of one human particularity or another. And, of course, the main particularity the postmodernists thought characterized much of Western academic work in the past is the particularity of

Eurocentric white males. Postmodernists thus tend to argue that particularist learning is all there is. On the postmodernist view, there should be many different particularities represented in a university, and it should be recognized that they are equally legitimate.

On a view such as this, the answer to the question whether Christianity and scholarship can mix is again a definite affirmative, but that affirmative answer does not mark a return to the old Christian tradition found in a preceding era. Instead, the idea is that Christianity and scholarship can legitimately mix because all scholarship, all intellectual endeavor, is only perspectival; and Christianity is one perspective among others. And so postmodernists recommend pluralism of perspectives. Proponents of a particular perspective should engage in reflective dialogue with the proponents of other particularities; and Christians, like everybody else, should be prepared to alter some of their beliefs in consequence of that dialogue.

Postmodernist views have generated considerable debate. That debate has called our attention to the difficulty of identifying the particularities that postmodernism wants to privilege. Consider in this connection the acclaimed African American philosopher Kwame Anthony Appiah. He was born in London to a British mother and an African father. His mother's father was the British ambassador to Moscow during the Second World War, and his father's family were part of the royal household of Ghana. He was largely raised in Ghana, but he took his undergraduate and graduate degrees at Cambridge. His mother was an elder in a nondenominational Christian church, and his father's family had ties to indigenous African religions. He himself has been employed for many years at New York University as a professor of philosophy and law. Now, if Appiah were to engage in particularist academic work in the university, what particularity would he belong to? How would he identify his particularity of nationality? Of race? For that matter, why suppose that race, for example, constitutes one particularity? As Appiah himself points out,[2] the experiences of Blacks in America are vastly different from the experiences of Blacks in Africa; and Black people in Africa themselves have a myriad of different languages, traditions, and histories. So it is not easy to decide what constitutes a person's particularity.

Appiah himself makes a case worth considering against the postmodernist position. He argues that something like a failure to accept the idea that there is one universal, generic human nature, in learning and elsewhere, is at the heart of all racism. In discussing the nineteenth-century Pan-Africanist Alexander Crummell, Appiah argues that those who make race a basis for grouping human beings into particularities are still racists of one sort or another, even if their intentions are benevolent rather than oppressive. He sums up his argument by saying,

> Americans need . . . to escape from some of the misunderstandings in modern discourse . . . epitomized in the racialism of Alexander Crummell. . . . [B]ecause the intellectual projects of our one world are essentially everywhere interconnected, because the world's cultures are bound together now through institutions, through histories, through writings, [Crummell in fact] has something to teach [not just Africans, as he thought, but rather] the one race to which we *all* belong.[3]

But what about the hope for the Christian perspective that postmodernism seems to imply? If Christianity is one particularity among others, Christian views have as much right to be presented in the university as any other particularity does. It seems that this privilege will be lost if postmodernism is rejected.

And yet if we look at the Christianity of Augustine of Hippo or Anselm of Canterbury or Thomas Aquinas or Martin Luther or John Calvin, for example, their Christianity is bolder and more demanding than this postmodernist particularist stance. It is not content with being an allowable particularity. It claims to be true, and true for everybody everywhere. What is wrong with the views of the atheist—on Augustine's views, for example—is not that the atheist fails to see Christianity as an allowable particularity but that he fails to acknowledge Christianity as true. Augustine certainly would have repudiated the idea that he was entitled to engage in learning as a person coming from one particularity among others. Augustine is more notable for his passionate conviction that Christianity provides the truth that is consciously or inchoately sought by everyone.

The importance of Augustine's attitude is brought home with memorable eloquence by the great nineteenth-century abolitionist and former slave Frederick Douglass. It is worth quoting him at some length:

> I love the pure, peaceable, and impartial Christianity of Christ; I therefore hate the corrupt, slaveholding, women-whipping, cradle-plundering, partial and hypocritical Christianity of this land. . . . I am filled with unutterable loathing when I contemplate the religious pomp and show, together with the horrible inconsistencies which everywhere surround me. . . . The man who wields the blood-clotted cowskin during the week fills the pulpit on Sunday, and claims to be a minister of the meek and lowly Jesus. . . . He who sells my sister for purposes of prostitution stands forth as the pious advocate of purity. He who proclaims it a religious duty to read the Bible denies me the right of learning to read the name of the God who made me. . . . The warm defender of the sacredness of the family relation is the same that scatters whole families, sundering husbands and wives, parents and children, sisters and brothers, leaving the hut vacant and the hearth desolate. . . . The slave auctioneer's bell and the church-going bell chime in with each other, and the bitter cries of the heart-broken slave are drowned in the religious shouts of his pious master.[4]

Douglass's fearsome denunciation of the Christianity of the slaveholders illuminates Augustine's ardent insistence on the authoritative truth of Christianity. If there were not one objective and authoritative truth about what is real and what is good in the world, then on what would Douglass's scalding scorn of the Christians of his time be based? For Douglass, it is the heritage of the Christian tradition which provides an ethical plumb line that makes perfectly clear the evils of those who thought of themselves as Christian and yet enslaved others.

So although postmodernism was intended to empower those who had been marginalized in the past, it is in fact not compatible with a robust program of social justice. If there is no acceptable basis for a person in one particularity to criticize the views of someone in a different particularity, it is hard to see how postmodernism can do much except support the status quo. So the postmodernist approach is worth rejecting in favor of the conviction, characteristic of the Christian intellectual heritage, that there is one truth, one truth even about ethics and theology, that holds universally for all human beings.

On the other hand, of course, Douglass's denunciation also makes forcefully evident the potent ability of moral evil to yield self-deception. The Christian intellectual heritage is helpful in this regard too. It takes no more than a modest acquaintance with this heritage to show the power of human moral evil to corrupt the minds even of those who believe of themselves they are committed to the Christian worldview. And without doubt, as postmodernists have argued, in the time when the modernist ideal of generic human nature governed in Western universities, the academy was in fact dominated by white Eurocentric males who supposed that their interests and values constituted the norm for all human beings and who treated others in biased or unjust ways.

Clearly, one safety against a malign tendency to self-deception lies in welcoming diverse perspectives. Augustine himself thought that heretics performed a valuable service for the church.[5] The church would never search out the truth regarding the faith so zealously, Augustine thought, if it were not driven to do so by its opponents. And so one of the best ways to strive for the Jesuit ideal in education is actually to welcome competing particularities in the academy and let them argue together. Even if postmodernism should be rejected, the promotion of pluralism in Jesuit universities is nonetheless a help toward the goal of handing on the Christian intellectual heritage.

Fr. Sosa is therefore right to emphasize intergenerationality as a significant part of the needed response to the current challenges faced by Jesuit college and universities. The Christian intellectual heritage transmitted from one generation to the next gives a Jesuit institution the grounding that enables its students, faculty, staff, and administrators to seek the truth of God and creation and to strive to transform society in the spirit of the Gospels. The Christian intellectual heritage is central to what the mission of a Jesuit college or university embodies and promotes, and the pluralist challenge to it is a safeguard against the kind of evil that has so often been done in the name of Christianity.

Interculturality: The Internal Challenge

Fr. Sosa's recommendation of interculturality, with its emphasis on pluralism, is therefore support for his recommendation of intergenerationality. But here a problem can seem to arise. That is because it seems as if there is a tension between intergenerationality and interculturality.

The tension arises, of course, because Christianity is an exclusive religion. There are many claims about God and about human beings that Christianity takes to be true, entirely true, literally true; and, according to Christianity, all those who reject these claims are simply mistaken. Augustine's sort of commitment to Christianity is not in good repute now among many academics because they see in it only arrogance.

It may help to see this problem more clearly by considering the argument against any kind of exclusivity made by the well-known American scholar Gordon Kaufman. Kaufman has argued that every proponent of an exclusivist worldview needs to understand and reflect on the significant implications of the plurality of religious traditions and claims. In his view, "what . . .

[is] required now . . . is careful and appreciative study [of a plu-
ralistic kind], together with an attitude of openness [toward all
worldviews]."[6] According to Kaufman, a commitment to pluralism in worldviews ought to lead to "a profound questioning of
the propriety of making dogmatic claims of any sort with regard
to . . . [the] ultimate 'reality' or 'truth'" of religious and philosophical traditions.[7] The crucial significance of religious pluralism from Kaufman's point of view, then, is that it contributes to
a kind of agnosticism about every worldview.

Furthermore, as Kaufman sees it, such pluralism entails more
sympathy with or respect for various other worldviews than an
Augustinian insistence on the truth of Christianity implies,[8] and
so it should leave people with "a deep humility about the religious and philosophical traditions [they themselves] . . . have
inherited."[9]

Now it is true that if the claims of a worldview such as
Christianity are true, then any claims incompatible with them
are false. So, by virtue of being committed to the truth of
Christianity, Christians are committed to judging that many
claims of other religions are false. And, Kaufman supposes, to
judge that the claims of other religions are false is to show oneself lacking in sympathy and respect for those religions.

But here it is worth noticing that rejecting some propositions
as false is just an essential consequence of the adherence to any
worldview. That Christianity stands by its own claims as true
and rejects incompatible claims as false does not single it out in
any way from other worldviews. Any coherent worldview, including Kaufman's own sort of agnostic pluralism, does the
same. Kaufman's position is committed to the truth of pluralism
and agnosticism; and so it entails rejecting not just the beliefs of
a particular religion but actually the beliefs of all worldviews and
religions when they differ from the beliefs of the agnostic pluralism that Kaufman himself holds. In particular, Kaufman's position must reject as false all the central claims made by
Christianity, Judaism, Islam, Hinduism, Confucianism, and
Buddhism, for example, because they are claims to know

something about the ultimate foundation of reality; and on Kaufman's view any such claims are, strictly speaking, false. If he is worried about a lack of sympathy and respect for worldviews other than one's own, then it is worth noticing that an agnostic pluralism is not more sympathetic and respectful with regard to other religions, but less.

Here it should also be noted, however, that sympathy and respect are attitudes that are shown primarily toward persons, and only in a derivative sense toward systems of belief. To have sympathy is fundamentally a matter of sharing the feelings of some person. To say that one is in sympathy with Marxism, for example, is to say that one is inclined to feel about things as committed Marxists do. But clearly one can reject a position without loss of sympathy and respect for the persons who hold it. It is possible to reject the worldview of some person and yet to feel great sympathy and respect for that person. It is a mistake to associate sympathy and respect with sharing beliefs or even with refraining from repudiating beliefs, as Kaufman seems to think. In fact, tying our sympathy and respect for persons to the worldviews they hold seems precisely the sort of mistake which has done the most to provoke the hatreds that the proponents of pluralism want to rule out.

These reflections show that the recommendation to intergenerationality is not after all inconsistent with the recommendation to interculturality. Any coherent worldview, including agnostic pluralism, has to take its position to be true and to reject claims inconsistent with its position as false. And doing so is perfectly compatible with respect and sympathy for others, no matter what worldview they hold.

These reflections would therefore be sufficient to ward off worries about taking the commitment to the Christian intellectual heritage as foundational for Jesuit universities if it were not for the fact that those who love any worldview will want others to share it. Out of their concern to share what they love, the many conflicts we ourselves are familiar with can arise again. The intergenerational commitment to the transmission of tradition and the intercultural promotion of plural, competing worldviews can consequently after all come into conflict.

And so one way to understand Fr. Sosa's charge to those with responsibility for Jesuit colleges and universities is as an exhortation to consider how those institutions can maintain the Christian intellectual heritage and yet also contribute to a society with justice and fraternal relations when the society is an amalgam of people coming from different cultures and committed to varying worldviews.

In this connection it is helpful to reflect on the life and work of the great Jesuit scholar and missionary Matteo Ricci. As Fr. Sosa recommends in his address, we can gain help in meeting the challenges of our times by considering the sort of person that Jesuit universities should honor and uphold as an exemplar. Matteo Ricci is and ought to be exemplary for all of us.

Ricci was born within the lifetime of St. Ignatius Loyola. During his formative years in the newly established Society of Jesus, he acquired expertise in the science of his time and also in its engineering skills. He had considerable knowledge of astronomy, for example, so that he was able to predict solar eclipses; and he had mechanical ability with the European-style chiming clocks of his day. He was also enviably literate in the Thomist philosophy and theology then central to study in the Society of Jesus.

The Christian intellectual tradition was handed on to him, and he gave his life to handing it on to others. While he was still in his twenties, he set out for China to evangelize the Chinese, to convert the Chinese to the Thomistic Catholic worldview foundational to the education he himself had received in the Society of Jesus. That Ricci even attempted this mission shows the power of his Jesuit formation. He left from Lisbon in 1578, and it took him until 1582 finally to make it to China. That arduous journey separated him for most of the rest of his life from all the people and places he had known before. The travel itself was fraught with risks and difficulties, and his time in China was marked by significant hardships.

In his commitment to his Jesuit foundation in the Christian intellectual heritage, Ricci accepted the philosophical theology of earlier centuries and devoted his life to transmitting it to the Chinese; but he did so with a remarkable respect for the intellectual and cultural riches of China. With very little help, Ricci taught himself Chinese and educated himself in the history and culture of China; in the process, he gained a stunningly impressive familiarity with the classics of Confucianism as well as with Buddhist and Taoist texts. And he put all this expertise in service of sharing the Christian intellectual heritage with the Chinese.

His scientific knowledge and mechanical abilities with clocks first brought him to the attention of the Chinese emperor; and his expertise in the classics of Chinese literature gained him the respect of Chinese intellectuals. His philosophical and theological skills helped him win over a number of the Chinese literati who dealt with him. In consequence of his labors, he was successful in his mission. The first Catholic church in China was built through his efforts, and those who came to it came because Ricci's work had inspired them to seek for themselves the greater glory of God.

Now, without doubt, in the history of Western missionary activity, there were Christian missionaries who used missionary activity as a cloak for imperialism and exploitation. The early history of Europeans in China is itself an example of the way in which an assumed superiority of Christian culture could enable serious injustice against other peoples. But Ricci's life and work illustrate one way to maintain the Jesuit commitment to the Christian intellectual heritage while respecting the lives and honoring the culture of others. Ricci was held in esteem by the Chinese nobles of his time not only because of his expertise in Western science and philosophy but also because of his willingness to learn from Chinese culture and his esteem for its achievements.

And so Ricci sets a standard for one way in which to fulfill Fr. Sosa's charge. He exemplifies the intergenerationality Fr. Sosa recommends, and he also illustrates the way intergenerationality can be combined with interculturality. Yet how did Ricci achieve this synthesis?

Here I think it is helpful to look briefly at Ricci's classic book *The True Meaning of the Lord of Heaven,* which was first published in 1603 and comprised his main attempt at evangelization through the written word. In this book, which Ricci wrote in the Chinese he had so laboriously acquired, Ricci used his expertise in the great Chinese texts to show that the Confucian worldview and Thomistic philosophical theology can together illuminate the world and the way to live well in it. It is worth noting that it was one of the Chinese literati who had become Ricci's friend who provided the financial support to print this book in China.

The True Meaning of the Lord of Heaven

Ricci's book is cast as a dialogue between himself and a Chinese scholar. After an introduction which Ricci writes in his own voice, the work opens with a statement by the Chinese scholar. As the Chinese scholar explains, he has heard that Ricci and his whole country worship only the Lord of Heaven; and he knows that, according to Ricci and his countrymen, the Lord of Heaven is the creator, sustainer, and provident governor of everything. But the Chinese scholar says that he himself has "heard nothing about these matters, and none of our wise men and respected scholars of former times has ever expounded them."[10]

So the dialogue opens in effect with a statement of the problem of exclusivity. Ricci's Chinese scholar claims that he and his fellow Chinese scholars have not heard of Ricci's God. But how could there be a true God who cared for all his people and yet did not make himself known to all people?

Ricci's response is to argue that the doctrine the Chinese scholar thinks he has never heard of is actually part of the Confucian worldview, as Ricci sees it. Ricci is no proponent of postmodernism. He definitely does not think that every Chinese worldview is on a par with the Christian intellectual heritage or that all Chinese worldviews are equally true. On the contrary, Ricci is explicit about his dislike of Taoism and Buddhism. But as he explains to the Chinese scholar in the dialogue, it is not necessary to suppose that every worldview is true in order to claim that a provident God has given all people knowledge of the truth about God and God's governance of the world. It is enough to hold that every people has available to it at least one worldview that does contain such truth.[11]

When it comes to the people of China, Ricci thinks that Confucianism is a vehicle for connecting the Chinese with the one true God. So he says, "He who is called the Lord of Heaven in my humble country is He who is called *Shangdi* (Sovereign on High) in Chinese."[12] Ricci goes on to quote a variety of Chinese sources to make this point, and he sums up his survey of those sources in this way: "having leafed through a great number of ancient books, it is quite clear to me that the Sovereign on High [that is, the Christian God] and the Lord of Heaven are different only in name."[13]

So the first part of Ricci's response to the concern raised by the apparent exclusivity of Christianity is to deny a good part of the exclusivity. The provident God who has made himself known to his people in the Christian intellectual heritage Ricci learned during his formative education by the Society of Jesus is the God who has made himself known to the Chinese as the Lord of Heaven. In this respect, Ricci thinks, God has not privileged Western Europeans over Eastern peoples.

Clearly, this is a surprising thing for a self-avowed missionary to say. Ricci is claiming, in effect, that the Chinese are already in possession of knowledge of the God Ricci came to China to teach the Chinese about. The names used by Confucian Chinese and European Christians are different names, Ricci says, but the ultimate reality spoken about, the God who is studied and revered, is one and the same. But if the Chinese already know, or are in a position to know, the same God Christians worship, what is the point of Ricci's evangelization?

Ricci has the Chinese scholar in his dialogue give the answer to this question:

> Those who recite the canonical writings merely read the words without being able to understand their purport. I once read the following words in the *Book of Odes*: "This King Wen, watchfully and reverently, with entire intelligence served the Sovereign on High, and so secured the great blessings. His virtue was without deflection." Now, having heard you discourse on the profundities of humanity and how you have related it to the Lord of Heaven, I understand for the first time what the writer of that ode had in mind: anyone who serves the Sovereign on High will not be lacking in virtue.[14]

According to the Chinese scholar in the dialogue, the Confucian ode he cites contains a view that Christianity also teaches; but the view is highlighted and made clearer in Christianity than in the Confucian ode, so that only after having seen the point in Christian teaching does the Chinese scholar recognize that that view is in fact in the Confucian ode.

On Ricci's view, then, although the provident care of God has put into Chinese culture the things necessary for an understanding of God, at least some of those things are only implicit. So one purpose of evangelism, according to Ricci, is to aid in making explicit what is present in the cultural riches of another people, but tacit or obscure without the help of evangelism.

On the other hand, of course, as Ricci himself knows, it is not possible for him to find every central Christian doctrine somehow inchoately presented in Confucian texts. So, for example, Ricci cites texts from the Chinese *Book of Odes* that apparently make explicit mention of heaven, a state of life after death in which the virtuous are happy. The Chinese scholar in the dialogue concedes that there is a heaven; he even concedes that heaven is in fact referred to in the *Book of Odes*. But he objects strenuously to the Christian doctrine of hell:

> When one investigates these classical texts, one finds that the sages of ancient times already believed that after death there assuredly was a place of joy reserved for the good. But you definitely cannot discover any reference to hell in the canonical writings.[15]

With respect to the Christian doctrine of hell, then, the Chinese scholar insists that Ricci's chosen strategy of finding the major doctrines of Christianity in Confucianism is useless.

Furthermore, the Chinese scholar argues that here at last Ricci is stuck with facing up to the insulting exclusivity of the Christian religion:

> Confucians regard the sages as authoritative examples [for the rest of mankind], and the sages used the canonical writings and their authoritative commentaries as media of instruction; but in all our canonical writings and their authoritative commentaries there is not a single mention of . . . hell. Are you trying to say that the sages were ignorant of this teaching? Why is it concealed and not mentioned?[16]

To this objection, Ricci proposes a methodological response with important implications:

> If one says that hell is not real because it is not referred to in the canonical writings, one will be making a great mistake. According to the method of disputation in Western learned academies, an orthodox book can prove the existence of a fact, but it cannot prove the non-existence of a fact. In the ancient canonical writings of our Western nations, . . . [there is] no mention . . . of the two emperors Fu Xi and Shennong. . . . We cannot prove from this that there was no Fu Xi and Shennong. . . . If this [methodological principle] were not so, would it not be

> possible to say that many countries of the West do not exist sim-
> ply because there is no mention of them in the [Chinese] records
> that give an account of Yu [of the Xia dynasty]?[17]

Ricci is here pointing out that not every significant or beneficial truth about the world will be known to every culture. So, he says, Christian canonical writings—that is, the Christian Bible—is silent about the two Chinese emperors Fu Xi and Shennong or, actually (as we ourselves might add), about anything having to do with China. Cultures have something to learn from one another, not in the sense that every worldview is equally true, but in the sense that the traditional core of even a true worldview is incomplete in some respects and able to be supplemented profitably with information found in other worldviews. On Ricci's view, a great deal of what is important to know about God and God's governance of the world is implicit (or even explicit) in Confucianism, but it is possible that a Christian evangelist can bring it to the fore or make it more readily understandable. But when Christian evangelism operates in this way, it does not seek simply to replace the Chinese cultural tradition with the Christian intellectual heritage. On the very understanding of God in the Christian worldview, God is the God of every people and provides for all of them, so that in every people's cultural tradition there is something that is true and good.

On the Christian tradition that Ricci inherited and tried to pass on to the Chinese, then, it is right to share Christianity with the Chinese. But, as Ricci thought, that very Christian tradition also implies that the providence of God has operated through the generations of Chinese culture to yield a Chinese tradition with its own individual goodness. As Ricci's book, in fact as his whole life, makes clear, this Chinese tradition struck him as highly admirable. And so he maintained his adherence to the Christian intellectual heritage he had learned in the Society of Jesus and had come to China to share; and, as he did so, he also learned to love the Chinese tradition that, he believed, was also a gift from the provident God the Society of Jesus was established to serve.

Conclusion

A full examination of the views expressed in Ricci's great book *The True Meaning of the Lord of Heaven* and a discussion of the controversy that his work engendered in the Catholic West would take much more discussion than is possible in this short response to Fr. Sosa's address.[18] But enough has been said, even in this brief exposition, to show that Ricci's position is sophisticated and promising when it comes to a resolution of what seemed to be a tension between Fr. Sosa's two recommendations of intergenerationality and interculturality. It is possible to take as the core of Jesuit education the Christian intellectual heritage that has been foundational for the Society of Jesus and that Matteo Ricci gave his life to share with others and yet to appreciate and value cultures and worldviews other than one's own. Intergenerationality and interculturality are not only compatible, as Fr. Sosa's address implies, but they are in fact complementary. The worldview accepted in the Christian intellectual heritage implies Ricci's attitude toward non-Christian worldviews. And so I can think of no better way to sum up these reflections on Fr. Sosa's stimulating address than by quoting the Magis prayer the German Jesuits gave to participants at one World Youth Day:

> God, our Father,
> You are always present with us,
> In our stillness and in our bustling,
> In our solitude and in our gatherings,
> In what we trust and in what is alien to us.
>
> Let us grow in recognition
> That you are here for us,
> That we can seek you in all things,
> That we will find you when we do.

You have sent us your Son Jesus
As hallmark of your presence.
Help us to know him more deeply,
That we may see the world as he sees it,
That we may value what he values,
That we may do as he does.

Fill us with your Holy Spirit
That we may love Jesus
More and more,
And more and more
Follow after him.

Notes

1. Thomas Aquinas himself maintained that there is progression in theological understanding, for example. See *Summa Theologica* II-II q. 174 a. 6 and q. 176 a.1 ad 1. I am grateful to Thomas Joseph White for these references.
2. Kwame Anthony Appiah, *In My Father's House* (New York: Oxford University Press, 1992), Chap. 1.
3. Appiah, 27.
4. See "Narrative of the Life of Frederick Douglass," *The Classic Slave Narratives,* ed. Henry Louis Gates Jr. (New York: Mentor Books, 1987), 326–27.
5. Augustine, *City of God,* Book XVI, chap. 2.
6. Gordon D. Kaufman, "'Evidentialism': A Theologian's Response," *Faith and Philosophy* 6, no. 1 (1989): 40.
7. Kaufman, 42.
8. Kaufman, 39.
9. Kaufman, 42.
10. Matteo Ricci, *The True Meaning of the Lord of Heaven (TTMLH),* revised edition, ed. Thierry Meynard, SJ, trans. Douglas Lancashire and Peter Hu Kuo-chen, SJ, Institute of Jesuit Sources (Boston: Boston College, 2016), 43.
11. Fr. David Suwalsky has reminded me to add that, of course, on Christian doctrine God also puts his law into the hearts of people; see, for example, Jer. 31:33. I am grateful to Fr. Suwalsky for helpful comments on an earlier draft of this paper.
12. Ricci, *TTMLH,* 95.

13. Ricci, *TTMLH*, 101.

14. Ricci, *TTMLH*, 317.

15. Ricci, *TTMLH*, 269.

16. Ricci, *TTMLH*, 268–69.

17. Ricci, *TTMLH*, 271. This edition of *TTMLH* prefaces the text from which this quotation is taken with a heading indicating that the quoted words are spoken by the Chinese scholar; but this is an obvious error in the edition not only because the text in question is a response to the immediately preceding words of the Chinese scholar but also because the quotation itself refers to such things as "our Western nations."

18. The editors of the *TTMLH* say that the controversy generated by Ricci's approach, which became known as "the Rites Controversy," and the reaction of the Roman inquisition in 1704 to the controversy "proved a major setback to the growth of Christianity in China for more than two hundred years" (27).

7

Making Our History

Catholic Social Thought and the Future of U.S. Jesuit Higher Education

DAVID J. O'BRIEN

Introduction

HISTORY HAPPENS, SOMETIMES WITHOUT US, sometimes to us, and sometimes with us. Jesuits know all about that. They have always wanted to make history, in part by helping others join them as historical subjects. As one Jesuit, Pope Francis, told his brothers in Argentina years ago, they got into education because they wanted their students, and everyone else, to know that things do not have to be as they are.[1] They, Jesuits, collaborators, students, they matter. History could be their story, and their responsibility. Across the world, and across the United States, that invitation to accept history-making opportunities, and responsibilities, is still being issued, most recently by Father Arturo Sosa to all of us who share in the ministry of Jesuit higher education.

In his address, Father Sosa noted that among the "tensions" facing each Jesuit college and university are the "tension between the history, the tradition that has made the institution what it is, and the challenges of the present crisis that open up an uncertain future." That sounds familiar. We in Jesuit higher education in the United States have long been negotiating that tension between memory and hope, usually in our own institution, occasionally together.

Higher education in the United States is one chapter of a long Jesuit tradition of accompanying people, young and not so young, into a "hope-filled future." With Pope Francis, Father Sosa suggests we have now arrived not just at "an epoch of change" but "a change of epoch."[2] Jesuit leaders have recently insisted that they wish to carry on their work "at the heart of human history."[3] Our discernment about where to go and how to get there, Father Sosa suggests, may require us to "let go of the reins," change our "focus and habitual ways of making decisions," and be open to "something new."

In Jesuit higher education in the United States, the Jesuits a half century ago began sharing power and responsibility; they no longer control "the reins." With their "collaborators" they have guided their colleges and universities through many changes, trying, always, as best they could, in Father Sosa's words, "in everything to love and to serve." Given the state of higher education, and the country, and the Church, something new is indeed coming, like it or not. The challenge set by Father General is to make some history, to take our share of responsibility for determining what that something new will be.

Recent History

Among the many "new things" we encounter as we consider a "change of epoch" is that the on-the-ground politics of Jesuit higher education have changed dramatically. Father Sosa says that, in ever-changing circumstances, "we [Jesuits] propose to animate institutions that are excellent because people who work, do research, teach and study in them find the conditions to lead lives with meaning, lives that advance toward fullness." I know from experience that I speak for many faculty and staff of Jesuit colleges and universities when I say that our Jesuit colleagues have done that and we are very grateful.[4] Certainly *"animate"* has been the strategy in recent years, as laypeople have taken charge of Jesuit colleges and universities. Jesuits and colleagues inspired by them offer the communities they serve Ignatian spirituality, pastoral care, rich resources from Jesuit intellectual and academic experience, and on each campus, at least a few talented Jesuit trustees, administrators, faculty, and staff devoted to the communities and institutions they serve.

But these are not family firms, with Jesuits and their closest colleagues in charge, and others welcome guests. All are welcome, and share responsibility for the life and work of the community.[5] Over time what Father Sosa calls animation was detached from control as, in his words, Jesuits worked in "collaboration" with others, always aiming at "solidarity." "In the present moment" he says, "we cannot even imagine educational institutions, or any form of apostolic work, without plural teams in which people of distinct vocations of service join with Jesuits. We also have experience with Jesuits collaborating in apostolic works initiated and directed by other institutions, groups or persons." So in American Catholic and Jesuit higher education, the politics of animation, what Jesuits would call their "way of proceeding," has clearly changed. Today our understanding of the "university education of the Society of Jesus" is already a "new thing," and it is still changing as we reflect on Father Sosa's message in light of Catholic social teaching.

Catholic Social Teaching

Catholic social teaching has two central themes, both deeply rooted in Christian faith: on the one hand, human dignity and human rights; and on the other, solidarity and the common good. Care for both, in society and in the Church, has been at the heart of Catholic thought and imagination, as well as modern Catholic social teaching. In practice, dealing with each generation's "present crisis," they have not always fit easily together. Pope Leo XIII in Rerum Novarum (1891) shared the Catholic resistance to the structures and ideologies of "modernity," but he held in check those Catholics who wanted an all-out condemnation of the secular state and industrial capitalism. Instead he stressed the human dignity side, supporting a living wage, labor unions (preferably under clerical supervision) and government social insurance, a safety net. Forty years later, after the slaughter of World War I and amid political instability and economic depression, Pope Pius XI in 1931 reaffirmed support for wages and unions, but in order to ease class conflict and insure the common good, he proposed the "reconstruction of the social order," offering a Catholic middle way between socialism and capitalism.

Reforms inspired by solidarity and intended to draw classes into cooperation around common goods were indeed backed by a number of authoritarian regimes and nationalist conservative movements in heavily Catholic countries. They were sometimes populist but almost always directed by antidemocratic political parties with limited respect for human rights. In contrast American Catholic social action leaders, whose immigrant, working-class people had a big stake in civil and religious rights, translated Pius XI's proposals into support for independent unions and professional associations, industrial democracy, and social welfare legislation, as did postwar Christian Democratic parties in Europe and South America.

The crimes of right-wing governments and the advent of the Cold War against communism led the Vatican and most Catholic social activists after World War II to back away from the systemic criticism and structural reform of Quadragesimo Anno to emphasize human dignity and human rights, a shift affirmed by the second Vatican Council (1962–1965) and applied with energy by Popes Paul VI and John Paul II. In the last decades of the twentieth century, the Catholic Church, long identified as a conservative force for political authority and social order, emerged across the world as a defender of human rights and advocate for the poor and marginalized. In the United States cautious Catholic criticism of capitalism and support for shared responsibility for "firms, industries, and professions" of the New

Deal era gave way to defense of the right of labor to organize, support for income redistribution to ease inequality, and, more cautiously, advocacy for civil rights.

In Latin America, liberation theology grew out of that reaffirmation of human dignity and human rights and post-Vatican II studies of Scripture. Its intellectual architects, Jesuits among them, called for a "preferential option for and with the poor" and recovered some of the earlier critical analysis of the overall political economy. They called for unspecified "systemic" or "structural" changes; some flirted with "revolution" but without an independent proposal for a new social order. As a result liberation theology, with its bottom-up pastoral strategies, offered a critical method of understanding social injustice and encouraged serious commitment to that "preferential option." It permanently changed the increasingly global church and Catholic social teaching. But, as with Catholics calling for systemic change back in the 1930s, it sometimes led to a dangerous middle ground between polarized politics and revolutionary and repressive violence. Keeping dignity and solidarity together remains one of, if not the central, challenges of Catholic social thought and imagination, and therefore to Jesuit academic and intellectual life.

Jesuit Leadership

Jesuit ministry has reflected these developments. Human dignity, one pole of Catholic social thought, has grounded the Society's worldwide advocacy for human rights and support for the poor and powerless, and in the United States support for social and racial justice and a strong safety net. This side of Catholic discourse wins admiration, especially when connected with on the ground service to those in need, for example, with migrants and refugees "on the border" and across the world. But that admiration fades when attention is called to the sources of suffering and the need for changes not just of policies but of structures and power.

Jesuit leaders like Father Sosa, since the 32nd General Congregation of 1974, have recognized that solidarity, care for the unity of the human family and the common good, is urgently needed to deal with issues of poverty and marginalization, migration, climate change, and a renewed nuclear arms race, but proposals to deal with these large systemic issues lack popular and political support here in the United States. Pope John Paul II's defense of human rights was widely admired, but his equally passionate appeal for a new international order to prevent war, which he called "a moral imperative" and "a sacred duty," was ignored, even by most Catholics. Similarly, in the United States, recurrent violence against African Americans is often interpreted as "institutional racism" caused by some combination of what Martin Luther King Jr. called "poverty, racism, and militarism." But almost all reforms are aimed at improving "race relations," as in diversity initiatives and personal and interpersonal changes. Recent popes and Jesuit generals speak clearly of the need for systemic change, but the dream of a new society where it is easier to do, and be, good stands in Catholic thought as a moral standard and long-range goal but without a strategy or a political— or pastoral—home. That contrast between analysis of systemic problems and modest reform constitutes another central problem in contemporary American Catholic social thought and action.

All of that could be discussed with reference to worldwide Jesuit efforts to implement the Society's dramatic 1974 preferential option for the poor and pledge to make the pursuit of justice an integral element of Catholic faith and practice. As we have noted, over the last half century American Catholic colleges and universities transferred responsibility from religious orders to independent boards of trustees, and their faculties and staffs became more professional, and diverse. Throughout those years Jesuit leaders have worked hard to persuade their collaborators that the option for the poor and the service of faith and promotion of justice should be central components of each institution's mission and identity. Father Sosa sums up the "specific contribution" of Jesuit universities as helping "to pave the way to a more just society with fraternal relations among persons, their cultures, peoples, and nations so that the common good orients the decisions of the global political economy."

As Eileen Burke-Sullivan details in her essay in this book, making that contribution has been a consistent goal since 1974, part of what we have come to see as essential to the Jesuit mission in education. But strategies to achieve that goal have been modest. Translating the need to build a more just and peaceful world into specific intellectual and educational projects and programs is shared work requiring attention to politics, the politics of higher education, the politics of religion, and, in our case, the politics of democratic self-government. "Through politics, meaning is given to social life." Father Sosa says. His clear acknowledgment of the importance of politics in this "new epoch" marks a genuine "new thing" in this ongoing project.

Pope Francis and Catholic Social Thought

As we examine this new emphasis on politics, it is well to look at how Pope Francis has deepened and extended Catholic social thought and imagination. His assessment of the "signs of the times" reflects his experience as pastor and bishop in Latin America, and his focus on the poor, especially migrants and refugees, grows from that pastoral experience and his engagement with liberation theology and its later outgrowth, the "theology of the people." Three themes of his homilies and commentary, reflected in Father Sosa's statement, are of special importance for American Catholics and for Jesuit higher education.

First, to Catholic emphasis on human dignity Francis adds almost daily references to "encounter," engaging people as we find them, listening to their stories, responding to their presence, not allowing pre-existing images and judgments to block relationships, to condition love. Jesuits and those working with them know this as *cura personalis*, welcoming colleagues and students as we find them. This personalism informs a great deal of Catholic pastoral reflection in recent years, deepening commitment to the poor, the stranger, the outsider; easing tendencies to rush to judgment; and placing cautionary limits on social action. Pope Francis brings up this theme of encounter in dealing with moral questions related to gender and sexuality, but it has long informed his approach to social questions as well. For example, he urges pastoral ministers to move out into the community, to acquire "the smell of the sheep." He also appeals to young people to encounter each other, to risk living by their deepest beliefs, to reach for their dreams. More broadly, he suggests the importance of the pastoral dimension of Catholic social thought and imagination, not only in our option for the poor but in our options to be faithful disciples and responsible citizens, together.

Second, Pope Francis adds to appeals for social and political action on behalf of justice a genuine love for the world, most notably in his encyclical *Laudato Si'*. Although it has deep roots in Catholic tradition, this call to love, not just change, our "common home" may be Pope Francis's most dramatic, and controversial, contribution to Catholic social teaching. Our Christian and Catholic imagination has been shaped by sharp boundaries between the sacred and the secular, the church and the world, Christian insiders and secular outsiders; and by persistent, self-serving denunciation by Christians of secularization and secularism.

Pope Francis's appeal for solidarity and shared responsibility in the face of urgent human needs draws on Vatican II's "Pastoral Constitution on the Church and the Modern Word." Instead of finding Catholic identity in "contending with the world," the Church seeks to break down barriers and bring the faith, hope, and love of religion into the heart of society, into the making of history. For Pope Francis this world is our world, given to us by God, made sacred by God's never ending creation, by God's incarnation in Jesus, and by God's ongoing presence as the Holy Spirit.

With Francis's help we come to think of Catholic social teaching as arising from within the human family, all of us, and embracing our common home as the world we are making, for which we all share responsibility. In this understanding of Christian mission amid the signs of the times the move of Jesuit and Catholic higher education from the edge to the centers of American life makes sense. Encounter reminds us of the need for love and pastoral care for persons we meet each day; solidarity reminds us of our call to take public, political care of one another and our common home, God's earth, and our common homes in the communities, the worlds, we are making each day. The Jesuits sometimes think of this as *magis*, drawn by God's love beyond our daily work toward an ever more "universal good."

The third Francis shift in Catholic thought, building like the others on Pope John Paul II and especially Pope Benedict XVI, is what can be called an evangelical turn toward scripture and the words and witness of Jesus. Those who have worked with Jesuits will be very familiar with this as spiritual guidance centered on the presence of God in the resurrected Jesus and the Holy Spirit. Historian John O'Malley, SJ, said that St. Ignatius, at the founding of the Jesuits, turned the Society outward in missionary service to the world and inward toward interior prayer.[6] Speaking in homilies and messages about encounter with God and with one another, and love for the world given us by God, Francis is following those paths.

This turn to the Gospel, gradually unfolding since the Second Vatican Council, has had a powerful impact on Catholic social teaching. The careful moral analysis of just war remains an important resource, but now Gospel nonviolence has moved to the center of Church teaching. Pope Benedict went so far as to enrich teaching on political economies by suggesting a Gospel-centered "economy of gift" as a possible vision for the human family. Pope Francis has followed this with the "economy of Francesco" informed by marketplace encounters and care for common, shared goods. In short, the emphasis on Scripture reintroduces a note of idealism into Catholic social thought and imagination. It also suggests that Catholicism can offer not just criticism, sometimes perhaps prophetic criticism, but also openings to constructive proposals for solving problems and fulfilling aspirations. We could add that we find similar ideas in the words and witness of Martin Luther King Jr. and the American Black Christian communities with whom he served.

Each of these developments with Pope Francis has special importance for American Catholics. Encounter suggests a nuanced understanding of American individualism, often treated as a moral problem but also as personal freedom and responsibility and, in freedom, a way toward voluntary conversion and commitment. Recognition of the human dignity and responsibility for all persons, rich and poor, insiders and outsiders, is a foundation for both Christian discipleship and democratic citizenship. So is the idea that the world, our world, actually matters. Immigrant, working class, sometimes very poor, Catholics, in the past and today, had reason to see themselves as outsiders and resent the discrimination and unfairness of the dominant American society. But Jesuits, their colleagues, and their students always were, or hoped to be, insiders, for whom American society would be their shared home and therefore their shared responsibility. Therefore Pope Francis's call to genuinely care for our common home should inform our American appropriation of Catholic social teaching. That love for our world might also recall earlier Catholic attention to the laity, to pastoral strategies centered on personal authenticity and interpersonal compassion but also on meaning and purpose in work and public life.[7]

And the evangelical turn calls attention to a truth long evident to historians of American religion and increasingly clear to Catholics: that in a society of religious freedom and religious diversity, evangelicalism is the default drive of Christianity. As ethnic and religious subcultures give way to various forms of social mobility, Christians, faced with new relationships and receiving a variety of doctrinal and moral messages, are less inclined to rely on official church teaching in their spiritual and public life. Instead, they tend to rely on Scripture, their own experience, personal conversion and reconversion to Jesus, small affinity communities—even if many continue to value the sacraments and respect priests and bishops. In social and political matters they are inclined to ask first, not "What does the Church teach?" but "What did Jesus say?" and "What would Jesus do?"[8]

Father Sosa and Jesuit colleagues confirm these themes of Pope Francis. First, there is an ever stronger emphasis on the option for the poor, to which the recent popes now add an equally strong commitment to nonviolence. Discourse about social responsibility has moved a few steps away from the application of natural law principals in specific settings, the approach of the U.S. bishops' pastoral letters of the 1980s, to a more foundational vision of the Kingdom of God as proclaimed in the Gospel. This may arise from a pastoral sense that Christian love is the central social message and faith and hope are needed, and can be a source of joy, as one considers the obligations of discipleship and citizenship.

There is also a renewed emphasis, drawn from experience, on hope grounded in memory, of aspirations that give meaning to personal, communal, and social lives. I and others have argued that American Catholic history for immigrant communities was shaped by "folk memories brought to bear on new aspirations." Catholic faith, often blended with ethnic peoplehood, sustained American aspirations, and framed family journeys from immigrant outsiders to American insiders. There are personal as well as public experiences of Father Sosa's "tension" between tradition and current challenges as, like earlier generations, we share in shaping that "uncertain future." Becoming "men and women for and with others" can be a choice not just for personal authenticity, but for "faith and justice" grounded in solidarity, because Christians actually believe the Kingdom will come, for all of us.

And Pope Francis's emphasis on encounter, welcoming and connecting with persons as they are, highlights the central role of pastoral ministry and the pastoral center of all ministry, including social ministry. Human dignity—and human rights and personal responsibility—along with solidarity—the common good and shared social and civic responsibility—are two sides of the same call to love God and neighbor. Catholic social engagement, therefore, is personal and public, discipleship and citizenship, one calling to be fully oneself and fully open to others. Catholic social teaching speaks with wisdom about important matters of social life, but it arises from faith and hope based on love, and thus must always have a pastoral component, a care for persons that is an integral element of the life and work and aspirations of Christians and their communities.

American Perspectives

I have always approached Catholic higher education and Catholic intellectual life in a somewhat different way than my Jesuit colleagues. For one thing I am an American historian, not a theologian, drawn to that vocation by at least a touch of civil religion. Most Catholic, or Christian, theologians begin work within, and often on behalf of, their community of faith. A Catholic historian of the United States might choose, as I did, to work within and on behalf of the people of the United States, with special attention to those Americans who are in some way their people. As a result, when I take part in conversations about Catholic and Jesuit matters in higher education, I am inclined to think about, and ask others to think about, our specifically American experiences and responsibilities.[9]

Most of our higher education institutions have not chosen to be confessional colleges, many of which have an honored place in our country's panorama of higher education. But as we have emphasized here, our Jesuit and most other Catholic colleges and universities made, and continue to make, different choices. They are, by tradition and choice, fully American, chartered by the states, recipients of public financial support (unlike Catholic elementary and secondary schools), open to applicants and staff of all religions and none, and committed to public service. In addition they have always shared the aspirations of the American

Catholic people, their students and their families, to participate fully in American life. And, especially since the 1960s, they have taken an active role, indeed sometimes a leadership role, in the politics of American higher education. So it matters that they are American, as well as Catholic, and in some cases Jesuit, colleges and universities.

I have argued that our colleges and universities have three intersecting sets of responsibilities, academic (higher education), civic (American), and religious (Catholic and Jesuit). These are related, but distinct, parts of each institution's "mission and identity." Negotiating the three has changed over the years. After years of emphasizing their students' capacity to enter the centers of American society, Jesuit schools added options for the poor and community service to their mission. Religious orders of men and women, Jesuits among them, transferred responsibility for their colleges and universities to newly independent, predominantly lay, boards of trustees. More and more faculty and staff were laypeople, not vowed religious, and academic professionals, involved in scholarly disciplines and professional associations. Since World War II, these schools also shared in government support for higher education, support essential for their expanding student populations. Civic and professional responsibilities, and institutional independence, sometimes raised anxieties with Catholic leaders and friends: Were the schools still truly Catholic?

Such discussions about academic, civic, and religious responsibilities are still going on, and differences will undoubtedly influence responses to Father Sosa's message. This is as it should be as graduates, like the faculty and staff, also face in conscience the same trio of professional, civic, and religious responsibilities. Despite its long history of "contesting" with modern secular society, Catholicism has always had rich resources our assisting its people to negotiate these tensions. At Vatican II the world's bishops, with the pope, set aside the Church's defensiveness and acknowledged solidarity and shared responsibility with other "men [and women] of this age." Affirming religious liberty and freedom of conscience and honestly confronting problems of social and religious differences amid the Cold War, the emergence of oppressed peoples from imperial rule, and persistent poverty and marginalization, the Church invited its people and their Catholic institutions to renewed consideration in light of their faith of those economic, social, and political responsibilities.

That is why "through politics, meaning is given to social life," the civic component of responsibility, is perhaps the most important statement in Father Sosa's address. The questions he raises are political in the broadest sense. I was attracted to my profession as an American historian by politics. When I began looking at the Church in the United States, past, present, and future, I found, a little to my surprise, politics. Through the peace movement and peace studies I learned that the alternative to war, and violent conflicts of all sorts, was politics. I had opportunities to work with the American bishops on some important projects whose development and uneven results were determined by ecclesiastical politics. I visited all then twenty-eight Jesuit colleges and many more Catholic colleges and universities, where I once again found that internal campus politics, the politics of the church, and the politics of higher education shaped each school's mission and identity. So, too, despite claims of innocence, did the politics of knowledge.

This experience suggests that the future of American Catholicism and its cultural and educational institutions will be determined in large part by organized, purposeful action, and its absence. In public life, our country needs not just good citizens who vote intelligently but a sense of thick citizenship that requires consideration of human dignity and the common good in households and neighborhoods, workplaces and civic spaces, and in faith-based communities and institutions. And religious communities, for their part, require a sense of thick discipleship where responsibility is personal but also public, and shared responsibility is a fact and not an option.

Catholic social thought and imagination are helpful in considering how to live out calls to discipleship and citizenship here in the United States. The twin themes of Catholic social teaching, dignity and shared responsibility, correspond to the major themes of American public life, the promise of equality and inalienable rights of the Declaration of Independence and the deliberate, cautious commitment to self-government of the Constitution. American political and social history could be, indeed has been, written as a dialectic between the democratic promise of the one and achievements, and multiple shortcomings, of the other. Equality and rights promised by the Declaration, once achieved, bring for those winning greater liberty a greater share of responsibility for the common life. And genuine shared responsibility for self-government requires the freedom and empowerment of democracy. But as students of Catholic social teaching as well as American history know well, human dignity and solidarity do not always fit together nicely. Each group's pursuit of happiness often conflicts with the pursuits of others: thus the unanticipated, and unwelcome, appearance of "factions," coalitions, parties. Pleas for cooperation, bipartisanship, depend in turn on pre-partisan recognition of human dignity and trans-partisan care, perhaps even love, for our common home. In their absence, as we learn so often in international affairs, only power matters. The American challenge of democratic self-government, the Catholic and Christian challenge of integrating human dignity and solidarity, and the higher educational challenge to place knowledge at the service of the human family are connected. This is the complex situation in which we respond to Father Sosa's vision and advice.

Recommendations, Several Modest and One Not

So what is to be done in American Jesuit higher education now that both American and Jesuit/Catholic components of the mission and identity of these highly independent colleges and universities must be freely affirmed by committed participants? These participants, Jesuit and lay, like their former students now in other walks of life, occupy positions as insiders with responsibilities, but usually they are not in charge. In that context I offer some practical suggestions, under the three headings of professional, civic, and religious responsibility, and a final plea for much more.

The Higher Education Context: (1) *Practice self-government*: Bring human dignity and solidarity home in academic self-government, recognizing the vocations of all participants. Make meaningful commitments to share power and responsibility in institutional decision-making, and carry these commitments into professional associations of faculty, staff, administrators, and trustees. Insure that all are familiar with the many public issues facing American higher education. (2) *Take vocation more seriously*: Insure continuing commitment to enabling all students, including professional and graduate students, to engage questions of meaning and mutual obligation, supported by a commitment to faith and justice, and help relate this study to career aspirations. Insure that ethics discussions include social as well as personal responsibilities and have the constructive as well as critical components required for genuine vocation. And be serious about considering the presence or absence of communities and organizations to help sustain vocation after graduation. (3) *Think and talk about the politics of knowledge*: Most American professional and academic associations began in the idealistic Progressive Era (1890–1920) with mission statements that stressed the need to insure that knowledge serve and not undermine the always precarious life of democratic self-government. With new technologies and accelerating interdependence, the production, sharing, and utilization of knowledge made universities and "learned professions" important centers of power—and responsibility. They remain just that today, now amid another "Gilded Age" somewhat like the one that helped to prompt Progressive Era reforms. This is treacherous ground, as polarized politics can do great damage in academic as in governmental affairs. But shared responsibility for knowledge and its uses has been basic to Jesuit reflection since Vatican II. Exploring how to engage others in higher education—and in society at large—in that reflection might be a defining contribution we can make together to American intellectual and academic life.

The American Context: American colleges and universities, including Catholic institutions, affirm human dignity for everyone and shared responsibility for the ongoing experiment in self-government. Jesuits and Catholics share a faith that should lead them to join fully in this American work. (1) *Take citizenship seriously*: Thick citizenship, sharing responsibility for all areas of public life, is the practical requirement of democratic self-government. Elected governments are required to insure that work serves the public interest, which requires competent and dedicated public servants, but that responsibility rests as well on all citizens. Considering social and civic responsibility in higher education is a necessity for building a democratic society. And that means incorporating study of politics, broadly understood, into research and teaching as well as cocurricular programs. It may also include convening public forums for dialogue on important public questions. (2) *Train for public work*: In the 1980s, Jesuit institutions played a major role in developing Campus Compact as a national network of support for community-based and service learning. At one point in its history, leaders recognized the widespread popularity of community service and added a developmental component to help students move "from service to citizenship." In short, preparing for the "public work" required by self-government could be part of higher education. This in no way undervalues community and public service but adds initiatives to use those learning experiences as a basis of understanding the requirements of citizenship in daily life and civil society. At the same time, many colleges and universities joined in public declarations of their commitment to assess and improve their role in civil society. This is partly a matter of civic intelligence, creating settings where people can carry out the informed dialogue seen as the foundation of democratic self-government, but all too rare in society at large. Then there are the many instruments for exercising shared responsibility: community organizations, labor unions, professional associations, interest groups, and reform movements. Study of the role of organization and of power and powerlessness in all areas of common life is as important as study and reflection on personal morality and community service.[10] (3) *Develop a "civic audit" to examine how the institution, its programs and practices, reflect institutional and community commitments to human dignity and solidarity.* The college or university, and its components, should simply carry out the regular assessment of its professional, civic, and moral obligations as expected for all citizens. This process could open creative ways to invite graduates to participate in community life, and it would place important, and often mishandled, work for "diversity, equity, and inclusion" in its proper context: to enable us to better carry out, together, our shared responsibilities for one another and our common home.

The Jesuit and Catholic Context: Here discussion in the last generation centered on the status within the Church of self-defined Catholic colleges and universities. One center point was Catholic theology, its place in the university, and the responsibilities of theological research and teaching in the life and work of the Church. These are matters of importance to Catholics and demand more attention in Catholic public life. But in the new landscape of American religion and higher education, these divisions are no longer appropriate sites of reflection on our responsibilities as Catholics in higher education. More helpful would be: (1) *Thick discipleship, comparable to thick citizenship:* Christian life and Catholic practice in free societies today have to do with daily life and historic participation and responsibility. The leaders of the U.S. Church, to their credit, have tried to assist their people to apply principles of human dignity and solidarity in elections. They once did the same in championing the cause of working people, as they still do in some sectors of the American Church. But since more and more Catholics have entered management and the professions, the meaning and responsibilities of work have been intellectually and pastorally neglected. A thicker, more comprehensive understanding of discipleship might draw more attention to spiritual, pastoral, and intellectual initiatives in academic disciplines and departments concerned with education for liberating and meaning-filled work. (2) *An "option for the laity"*: On the foundation of thick discipleships, Jesuit academics and their lay Catholic partners could make a contribution by making an option for the laity comparable to the option for the poor: a way of seeing what is going on; an orientation to support and assist, be with and for, laypeople; and to encourage research and teaching that would strengthen and support so-called "secular life." Once again the landscape of the "new epoch" suggests the Church (and all faith communities) might direct pastoral strategies toward the community's status on weekdays at work and evenings in communities and at home, and then on its status when gathered for worship and prayer. (3) *Prioritize the pastoral*: All of this rests on a principle drawn from American Christian experience: In a free society, with multiple religious options, and with the challenges and opportunities provided by changes in America's culture and political economy, *pastoral ministry is the basic ministry, and all ministry must have a pastoral dimension.* For Christians in higher education, private or public, "campus ministry" is everyone's vocation.

Magis

A lot more is needed. These recommendations are practical in that they can meet some current needs of American colleges and universities. But they hardly address directly the pressing issues of violence, economic injustice, environmental disasters, migration and refugees, "modernization" of nuclear arsenals, and declining confidence in faith, reason, and democracy. Father Sosa, with Pope Francis, is right to place these major threats to the human family and our common home at the center of our reflections on faith, justice, higher education, and Catholic intellectual life. From now on, Jesuits and their collaborators in and out of colleges and universities might find the need for something more after reflection on Father Sosa's address and on the fiftieth anniversary of the 72nd General Congregation.

Jesuits now serve, but do not direct, the colleges and universities they founded, and they have wide responsibilities in Church and society. They have parishes and missions across the country, and schools, including the remarkable network of Nativity and Christo Rey middle and high schools. They are active in social ministries, including work with refugees and asylum seekers, and they offer important publications including *America* magazine. I was often disappointed that there were only limited efforts to connect Jesuit college and university resources with other Jesuit work, especially in social ministry. In addition, Jesuit self-understanding, as expressed in public documents like Father Sosa's, suggests strong support for more open consultation and shared responsibility in the Church, for ecumenical and interfaith dialogue and cooperation, for intelligent management of Church ministries, and for overall Catholic intelligence and imagination. But like other Catholic colleges and universities, Jesuit institutions have stood at some distance from the public life of the American Catholic community. Unfortunately, when the American Catholic community experienced genuine crisis over sex abuse and cover-up, Jesuits like almost everyone else concluded that dealing with it was up to the bishops and, in their case, religious superiors. It is not surprising then that the Jesuits, along with the community at large, have limited, "by invitation only" access to assisting their Church in recovering its unity, internal strength, pastoral, and public trust.

In 1991 in celebration of major Jesuit anniversaries, American Jesuit leaders established the National Seminar on Jesuit Higher Education to help Jesuit colleges and universities strengthen their sense of Jesuit and Catholic mission. I had the privilege of serving on the initial seminar. We considered establishing a "think tank" to assist serious study of mission-related questions but instead chose to publish a magazine, *Conversations on Jesuit Higher Education*, with essays analyzing specific issues to serve mission-related reflection on each campus. Conversation—dialogue among increasingly diverse faculty, staff, and stakeholders—seemed the appropriate foundation of mission-related work. Visits to campuses and impressive discussion with leaders and staff persuaded us that each institution had its own history and culture so that local reflection and action would be more helpful than analytical papers from a think tank.

More than two decades later, I was asked to reflect on that earlier decision, and, conscious of the emerging "new epoch" and the dramatic changes in church and society, I suggested that now a think tank serving American Catholic intellectual life might be needed. With the Church no longer managed well from the top down, with democratic self-government in danger, with massive structural challenges facing the human family, and with higher education facing serious questions about research, teaching, and cost, conversation, dialogue, remains essential but is not enough. Systemic, structural problems are real, they are global as well as national, and we are having a very hard time facing them, much less developing and implementing effective responses. The initial agenda of a Jesuit intellectual life think tank might focus on Father Sosa's appeal to help find "meaning in public life" and "contribute to the deepening and expansion of democracy."

Conclusion

So "something new" is surely needed for the "change of epoch." Finding it is work to be done together. Jesuits and their friends—freed from holding on to "the reins" of institutions, enriched by Christian faith and hope, and the love so many feel for their schools—might well be able to make a difference. History is being made, more rapidly and less humanely than we might like, and the need for serious people who believe things do not have to be as they are has never been greater. The work of a generation of remarkable academic leaders has helped bring Catholic intelligence and imagination, and Catholic higher education, to a point where the community's rich resources are available for service to the Christian movement, American democracy, and the human family and its common home. The next chapter remains to be written, and that chapter will be determined by religious faith, conversation and commitment, and, yes, purposeful politics, ours.

Notes

1. See lectures to Jesuit educators in *In Your Eyes I See My Words: Homilies and Speeches from Buenos Aires*, I (New York: Fordham University Press, 2019). My attention was called to this by theologian Matthew Ashely in a talk on Ignatian spirituality.

2. I have examined this setting of a "new epoch" in "Reflections on American Catholic History" in Hugh F. Crean, *Along the Way: The Life, Lessons and Legacy of Father Hugh F. Crean*, ed. Mark Stelzer (Kansas City: Andrews McMeel Publishers, 2023).

3. This is from the Jesuit Apostolic Preferences, https://www.jesuits .global/uap/

4. I served as a member of the initial National Seminar on Jesuit Higher Education and over the years visited all of the then twenty-eight American Jesuit colleges.

5. This is a crucial reminder for all discussions of Jesuit—and Catholic—mission and identity. For one of the best discussions of Catholic mission and identity see James Heft, SM, *The Future of Catholic Higher Education* (New York: Oxford University Press, 2021) and my respectful and extended reminder of the facts of diversity in academic communities and governance in the online journal ZEAL 1, no. 2 (2023). https://zeal.kings.edu/zeal/article/view/37

6. Cristiano Casalini and Alessandro Corsi, "John O'Malley and Jesuit Education: A Journey into Humanism," *Jesuit Higher Education: A Journal* 11, no. 2, Article 7 (2022): 24–37. https://epublications.regis .edu/jhe/vol11/iss2/7/

7. Philip Gleason in his magisterial history of American Catholic higher education *Contending with Modernity* (New York: Oxford University Press, 1995) properly emphasizes the way Catholic higher education leaders discussed "Catholic" identity in terms set by the pre-Vatican II ultramontane rejection of "modernity," a stance that fit well with the piety and practice of the American Catholic subculture. But the colleges and universities also worked hard to enable their graduates to make their way in American society while affirming their

own sense of shared responsibility for American public life. This distinction between personal and community commitment to Catholic faith and practice and shared responsibility in the political economy was a pastorally informed response to America's experiment in democratic self-government.

8. This argument is based on lifetime attention to changes in U.S. Catholic piety and practice assisted by the work of scholars like Mark Noll and Nathan Hatch. See, for example, Hatch's *The Democratization of American Christianity* (New Haven, CT: Yale University Press, 1991). And I have made the case in my *Isaac Hecker: An American Catholic* (New York: Paulist Press, 1992), especially in the last chapter and in essays on Hecker.

9. See my *From the Heart of the American Church: Catholic Higher Education and American Culture* (Maryknoll, NY: Orbis Books, 1994).

10. There were Declarations on Civic Responsibility complete with pledges of civic audits from presidents of research universities, the Wingspread Declaration, and later from presidents of colleges connected with Campus Compact. These are printed and discussed among other places in the *Journal of Higher Education Outreach and Engagement* 16 (2012), 235–68 and https://compact.org/resources/presidents-declaration-on-the-civic-responsibility-of-higher-education. Harry C. Boyte advised on these and wrote of citizenship in *Awakening Democracy Through Public Work* (Nashville, TN: Vanderbilt University Press, 2018).

ABOUT THE CONTRIBUTORS

Michael J. Garanzini, SJ, is the president of the Association of Jesuit Colleges and Universities. Fr. Garanzini was president of Loyola University Chicago from 2001 to 2014 and secretary for higher education for the Society of Jesus from 2012 to 2021. His area of specialization is religion and psychology with an emphasis on children and family dynamics and counseling.

James P. McCartin is associate professor in the Department of Theology at Fordham University, where he also leads a program designed to help faculty at various stages in their careers to explore how engagement with Jesuit mission may enhance their work. He serves as the chair of the National Seminar on Jesuit Higher Education, which publishes *Conversations on Jesuit Higher Education.*

Arturo Sosa, SJ, has served as superior general of the Society of Jesus since his election to that post in 2016. A Venezuelan by birth and a political scientist by training, he entered the Jesuits in 1966 and later served as rector-president of the Universidad de Frontera in Venezuela and as provincial superior of the Jesuits' Venezuelan Province. As a leader in Latin American higher education, Sosa organized a network of Jesuit institutions across twenty-one countries to expand access to higher education, especially to those who come from impoverished backgrounds. Under his direction, the Jesuits and their collaborators have emphasized Four Apostolic Preferences: showing the way to God through the Spiritual Exercises and discernment; walking with the excluded on a mission of reconciliation and justice; accompanying young people in the creation of a hope-filled future; and collaborating in the care for our common home, the Earth.

Eileen Burke-Sullivan (1949–2024) was vice president emerita for mission and ministry and professor emerita of theology at Creighton University. She is the author (with Kevin F. Burke, SJ) of *The Ignatian Tradition* and (with Michael G. Lawlor and Todd A. Salzman) of *The Church in the Modern World:* Gaudium et Spes, *Then and Now.*

James Hanvey, SJ, is secretary for the Service of Faith at the Curia of the Society of Jesus and serves as a consultor to Arturo Sosa, SJ, superior general of the Society of Jesus. Previously, he served as master of Campion Hall, Oxford University, and as a member of the theology faculty of Heythrop College, University of London.

Gordon Rixon, SJ, is president of Regis College, University of Toronto, where he joined the theology faculty in 1996 and where he serves as a research scholar at the Lonergan Research Institute. He has published extensively on an array of theological topics, including reconciliation, mysticism, and Ignatian spirituality.

Jennifer Abe is professor emerita of psychological science at Loyola Marymount University (LMU), where she also served as senior research associate in the Psychology Applied Research Center. She previously served as vice president for diversity, equity, and inclusion and associate dean of Bellarmine College of Arts and Sciences at LMU.

Eleonore Stump is the Robert J. Henle, SJ, Professor of Philosophy at Saint Louis University. Originally trained as a specialist in medieval philosophy, her most recent books are *The Image of God: The Problem of Evil and the Problem of Mourning* and *Grains of Wheat: Suffering and Biblical Narratives.*

David J. O'Brien, a U.S. historian, is Loyola Professor of Roman Catholic Studies Emeritus at the College of the Holy Cross and former University Professor of Faith and Culture at the University of Dayton. He is the author of many books, including *From the Heart of the American Church: Catholic Higher Education and American Culture.*